How to
Write a Poem

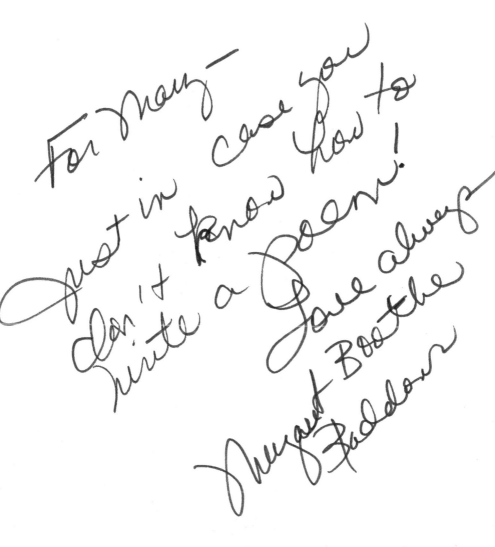

For Mary —
Just in case you
don't know how to
write a Poem!
Love always
Margaret Booth
Haddour

How to Write a Poem

Lawrence Jay Dessner
III

Washington Mews Books
A Division of New York University Press
New York • 1979

Copyright © 1979 by New York University
Library of Congress Cataloging in Publication Data
Dessner, Lawrence Jay.
    How to write a poem.

    1. Poetics.   I. Title.
PN1042.D47   808.1   78-65447
ISBN 0-8147-1766-7
ISBN 0-8147-1767-5 pbk.

Manufactured in the United States of America

Acknowledgments

Most of the poems in this book were written by students in my classes at The University of Toledo. I have revised them, lightly in most cases, to suit my purposes. The invented characters who appear as authors of particular poems bear no relationship whatever to the actual authors of the poems. They are entirely imaginary. The following student authors asked to be named: Robert A. Bernhoft, Jr., Jeff Bush, Mary Pat Carroll, Paul E. Coon, Richard D. Dorn, Karen Ferrenberg, Russell H. Hassen, Karen Fry Imhoff, Linda Meilink, Thomas G. Newton, Rheta P. Price, Michael Sares, Jane Schramm, Kathryn Sherman, Ray Sherman, Lois Daken Sumser, John Walczak, Sonja L. Waldeck, Cherie Jo Williams, and Mamie L. Williams.

Much of this book was written while on sabbatical leave from the University of Toledo during the winter quarter of 1978. I acknowledge with gratitude the award of that leave.

This book is dedicated to Phyllis, who loved it when it needed to be loved.

Contents

PREFACE

For Professors Only

Several years ago, one of my colleagues, an experienced teacher and scholar, appeared at the end of the corridor outside the English department offices, and approached with unusual alacrity the group of English professors, myself included, who were engaged in conversation there. It was obvious that he was going to regale us with some delicious tale of undergraduate innocence or administrative malfeasance, the two major themes of corridor chatter. As he neared, one could tell from the gleam in his eye and the curve of his latent smile that it would be in the former category. He had just left his class, he told us, a section of a sophomore humanities elective, Introduction to Literature. The course is strongly recommended to virtually all of the university's undergraduates, their first, and for most of them their last, college level course in literature. Pharmacists in training, engineers, premeds, predents, social scientists, and hordes of toilers in the sweet vineyards of Business Administration, come to that course, under duress, to take their ease after the rigors of the subjects they like to describe as "real." My colleague leisurely told his tale.

He had started his flock on poetry, and this day, before moving on to fiction, had made his usual exhortation on the importance of poetry, his last effort at vigorous though not optimistic proselytizing. As many of us have learned, Marvell's "Coy Mistress" is as good bait as we have, and our middle-aged mariner had walked his class through it with patient thoroughness. His explication finished, he paused, as dramatically as he could, and then, imagining himself a younger Richard Burton, had declaimed the poem nonstop, at its normal pace and with full rhetorical emphasis. He ended his performance with a panning survey of his upturned faces, a one-handed snap of the book in his outstretched palm, and an abrupt departure. "Take that," is what he meant by it all, "take that, you sniveling numbskulls." He strode across the front of the room, head high, like Alan Ladd marching off to his plane on his last suicide mission. But at the door he found his path blocked by a lumbering student who had, miraculously, known what was coming, and who had nimbly intercepted our hero. Amid the shuffling of chatter and clothing, the swell of the sounds of youth, the intrepid student had leaned forward to his mentor, blinked twice, and asked the following question, which is reproduced here in a faithful translation into the Queen's English: "Is there a book or a magazine which tells you how to write a poem?"

We did not stay for an answer to that ludicrous question. My own laughter must have rung a bit hollow, and I felt the group's attention turning toward me. After all, I had recently become the department's official teacher of Creative Writing, and the best part of the joke we had just heard was that I was its butt. And the suspicion that I was secretly of the devil's party was not entirely ill-founded. I was in fact engaged in answering the unspeakable question the lumbering student had blurted out, and I had begun to ponder writing the very book he sought. The book I intended, now, more or less, exists. My secret, in all its hideousness, is a secret no longer. And at my back I always hear a roar of mocking laughter and a crackling current of whispered derision: "He is teaching *them* to write *poetry*. All his talk about Creative Writing being a good way to learn about *literature* was baloney. He isn't lying to *them*; he's been lying to *us*. Is there a way to rescind his promotion?" To that angry chorus I have no retort. But to those who view my defection with sorrow or puzzlement I would offer some justification.

I did not set out to formulate mechanical prescriptions or in any way to design a syllabus for Creative Writing. My students are shown some good poems and are asked to listen to my praise of them. Their own early efforts, distributed to the class on mimeographed sheets, are criticized by me in painstaking detail and with painful frankness. "How *not* to do it," discouraging as that is for all of us, is the name of our game. But, as I read the stacks of comments students wrote in evaluation of the course, I began to notice not only their desire for explicit directions for writing poems, but the request that I provide such directions at the beginning of the course, rather than toward its end! Evidently, students thought that I knew "how to do it" and that I had been, perversely, withholding that invaluable information from them.

It is an article of faith with us all that the workings of our language and of our imaginations transcend the crass simplifications of technology. There are no equations here, no laboratory procedures to be followed with care in the belief that a successful result is assured. What on earth could I have been saying that led my students to think otherwise? How should I feel about the young woman for whom the humanities remains a dead letter, who devotes her energies and her aspirations to the arts of Certified Public Accounting, who leaves my class with a charitable B and these words: "The class was very worthwhile. We learned how to write poems. Now that I know how to do it, I expect I will write poems all through my life. Thank you."? Twenty versions of that give one pause.

There has been another disturbing surprise for me. Invariably, in each class of some twenty-five students, one or two write poems as good as the typical contribution to many academic literary periodicals. A few more students show promise of doing as well. It is a rare student who does not write at least a single poem that he knows is superior to those embedded in the song lyrics he has admired or to the verse of writers it pleases the mass public to think of as poets. (I say "superior" without qualification and based on my application of orthodox criteria.) Even with their rough edges, and their severely limited range of reference and vocabulary, not a few of the poems written in my classes have been bona fide works of art. This should not be. Art, as Matthew Arnold long since convinced me, is the fruit of culture. Culture is the sine qua non, and almost without exception my students come to me utter strangers to literary culture. They read nothing or next to nothing—not *Newsweek,* not the daily newspaper, not the college catalogue. They have neither read, nor thought about the acts of reading and writing. It is common for students to dispute this, to assert, truthfully, that they do read, science fiction often these days, but they are unable to name any of the titles or authors of the books they have read. It is not that they read paperbacks from which the covers and title pages have been removed. They do not think of books as things with names and as the products of identifiable persons. They assume that books and poems are like automobiles, existing uncaused, or without discoverable cause. The students do not lift the hoods of their cars.

Despite all this, they write poems and believe that I help them to do so. My own belief is that "innocence" and "culture" are problematic terms. Students come to Creative Writing for a reason they do not cite on questionnaires or articulate to themselves. Somewhere in the cultural desert of their lives they have been touched, in art's special ways, by some form of art, however rudimentary or meretricious, by a story, by a string of melodious or stirring syllables, by a turn of musical phrase or some graceful movement of mind or hand or heart. The "instinct for self-preservation" on which Arnold founded his wistful hopes is, however submerged, alive. The aesthetic experience leaves its mark and creates its need. And writing, of all the arts, is generally assumed to have no technology to be mastered, no tedious apprenticeship to be undergone. Just do what the man said: look in your heart, and write. Enrollment in college courses in Creative Writing is booming.

I have no qualms about cooperating with these accidents of history, nor am I embarrassed about casting some of my notions about poetry into a mechanical set of instructions, a paint-by-the-numbers kit for literature. After all, my students were themselves translating my unpremeditated comments into a system. I do not find it pleasant to contemplate what harm to the estate of poetry this book may do, insofar as it is known only by its title—and there are other charges to which I feel open. It may well seem that what I urge my students to see as poetry excludes a good deal of the world's great poetry. I do not think my "system" is at fault in this regard, but there is no question that students using it tend to write poems within a narrow band of the larger spectrum. I will not defend my part in this regrettable limitation. Nor will I plead innocent to charges of unacknowledged borrowings from my betters. There *is* nothing new in this book. While in the grip of the classroom's fine frenzy, I may feel quite otherwise. In tranquillity I have no doubt that it is all old wine in new bottles—or in pop-top aluminum cans!

CHAPTER ONE

Introduction

Hello! I'm very glad you're here. (I am smiling.) It would be better if I could see you, have you here to look at while I talk. It would be better if you could ask questions, and, later on, argue with me. It would be better if the poems we read and work over here were the poems you've written, but we will both do the best that we can. That will have to do, and it *will* do.

We have something in common, an interest in writing poems. And we know that this is a supremely important thing to do. We do not talk about the reasons for this great importance, even to each other, and I will not embarrass you or myself by stating the reasons, but neither will I, or you, forget that what we are doing here matters very deeply. Knowing that, and out of courtesy, we will pretend that we do it just for fun.

Before I go any further let me confess that the order of the following chapters is arbitrary and perhaps confusing. Each chapter says the same thing, and each says everything that I have to say about our subject. The only reason there is more than one chapter is that there are many ways to say what the book's title promises to say: "How to Write a Poem." Which chapters say it so that you will learn what you have come to learn you will find out only as you go along. If the rules I give you in the early chapters make sense and help you understand me, fine. If not, fine too. Shop around and take whatever versions of my story you like. I would be surprised to learn that anyone liked all of them. If you notice that I contradict myself from one chapter to another, good for you. It is the nature of the beast that various descriptions of it will contradict each other. If what I say about poetry is in violent opposition to what *you* think about it, or what other people have told you about it, *believe me!* For as long as you and I are together under the roof of this book, take my word for the general principles. When you leave, having learned or not learned what you came for, I claim and ask for no further submission to my dogmas. You will be unharmed and utterly free to believe what you will. In the meantime, consciously and deliberately suspend your disbelief. It may help you to know that what I tell you about poetry is not my personal theory but my ways of saying what everybody who knows about poetry assumes to be the truth of its nature.

This book has another peculiarity. I talk to you as if you were a single person standing before me. I give you orders, but I am not sure I should expect you to follow them immediately and unquestioningly. If you can do so, fine. If not, that may be fine too. There are as many ways to learn as there are ways to teach. The point I want to make is that nobody will learn how to write poems without actually writing them. Talk is easy, and cheap. Maybe amusing. I want to promise you that if you do what I say you will learn how to write poems that are good and that you will know are good. I do make that promise to you. But I ask you to do more than just read this book. I ask you to write poems and correct and revise them as I correct and revise the poems that appear in this book. And I ask you to be as tough a critic of your own poems as I am of the poems presented here.

This book is probably misleading in another way. I have tried to write it in as friendly and agreeable a manner as I can. I hope you find reading it entertaining, but I am afraid that if you do you may take what I have to say less seriously than I want you to. This book is not as easy as I am trying to make it sound. It is not like those do-it-yourself manuals in which a professional author leaves out things because he is addressing an audience of beginners and amateurs. There are many subjects—plumbing, chemistry, automobile mechanics—in which students must begin with elementary lessons and proceed slowly and in predetermined steps toward higher levels. No one can begin to study advanced physics, for instance, unless he has worked through elementary and intermediate physics. Often the elementary-level instructor ignores complications, even falsifies his subject so that the elementary student can learn elementary principles and operations more easily. Part of what you learn as you progress in such subjects is that what you were first taught was wrong.

Literature is one of the subjects that is different. There is no such thing as elementary literature. Even at the most elementary adult level, students of literature read and study the same works of literature as do the most advanced professional students. If this book were an introduction to literature, my examples would be selections from the world's great authors. As it is, my examples are by relative beginners, by college students in my undergraduate courses in Creative Writing. That is because this book is about *you*, about *your* creative writing, *your* literature. Since I cannot print the poems you have not written yet, I use the next best thing: poems by other beginners. But this book is not a book for beginners except in the sense that we are all beginners in this field. I have neither left things out nor rigged things because my readers are not famous poets or professors of English.

For all this to work, for a book addressed to beginners to convey the full and unadulterated story, its audience of "beginners"— that's you—must be prepared to work harder than they might have expected. It is not a matter of looking up words in a dictionary or of underlining and memorizing key passages. Your job is simply to not allow yourself to get lost. If a sentence does not make sense to you, if a discussion strikes you as boring or over your head, do not skim it and go forward—go backward! Especially in the discussions of details of particular poems, do not allow yourself to miss anything. Conscientiously, keep turning back to the poem itself and make sure you know what's being said about it. Read each poem, when it is first presented, with great care and patience. Study it, so that when it is discussed you will come to that discussion with ideas of your own. That is the price of admission.

Rule 1: Write a poem. I am not kidding. Write a poem. I need your poem in order to show you the other rules in operation. Close the book and write a poem. Or, if you have already written one, go get it. (Okay, that's a bit of kidding. *You* need your poem in order to compare it to the ones printed here.) While you are writing your poem, I will get a few poems students have turned in to me after I have given them only this first quite silly but absolutely essential rule: *write a poem*.

CHAPTER TWO

Getting Started

Welcome back, and congratulations. I am not kidding. You have followed Rule 1 and written a poem. Many people never get that far. They want to talk about being a writer; they love to talk about it. (That's what the old lady said to the priest when he asked her why she had just confessed to him an act of adultery she committed fifty years earlier.)

The writers of the following poems have also obeyed Rule 1, but they have broken quite a few other rules while they were about it. Of course they cannot be blamed for breaking rules they had not been given, and I will try to remember that when I use their poems to show you how my rules work. But I have the unfortunate habit of getting angry when I see a bad poem, and of appearing angrier than I really am. I am not angry at these writers, nor am I angry at their poems. (How can anyone be angry with or at a poem?) I think I am angry at the waste. These people, for all their years of living and schooling, don't know a poem from a pitchfork. How awfully their world has neglected them! We must start to do something about that.

I hope you will read these pretty awful poems with care. Even if your own poem is much better than these, these deserve and will repay some attention. It is a rare writer who is never in danger of forgetting the basic rules these authors do not know.

The writers of these dreary poems have shattered more rules

than I can think of. If you didn't know better—as I do—I wouldn't blame you at all for thinking their authors, as well as these poems, hopeless. Nobody is hopeless. To look away in despair, or out of courtesy, is to discard not only the poems but their authors—and that is something *we must never do*. That may strike you as a good rule for people as well as for poems. It is, in fact, when turned around a bit, Rule 2: Never treat your reader without respect. Let me list some of the ways this rule can be made more specific:

2.1 Do not lie to your reader.
2.2 Do not expect your reader to believe anything you don't believe yourself.
2.3 Do not waste your reader's time.
2.4 Do not confuse your reader.
2.5 Do not force your reader to guess about what's going on in your poem.
2.6 Do not speak to your reader as if you were Moses just returned from an exclusive interview with the Management.
2.7 Do not attempt to tell your reader how he should behave. You are a poet, not a guidance counselor.
2.8 Do not show off.
2.9 Do not boast.
2.10 Do not use unfair tactics to force your reader to say he likes your poem.
2.11 Do not attempt to take advantage of your reader's weaknesses.

This is far from all the ways Rule 2 can be broken. The rule generates enough regulations to run an army. Don't memorize any of them—but don't disobey any of them either.

It is not much fun to point out some of the ways these poems break Rule 2, but it is not supposed to be fun at all—no more fun than doing an autopsy. And we must not forget, as we cut away, what it is we are cutting. The poems before us are the best their authors could do to say what was important to them and to discover what was important to them. Let us operate.

Getting Started

Just for Fun

Fancy feathers, shades of green, flying	1
free, 'til hunter's gun is seen,	2
BANG!	3
Down	4
it	5
falls,	6
shades of Red.	7
Twisting,	8
turning,	9
fluttering, flashing,	10
earth-reaching,	11
crumbled,	12
still,	13
DEAD!	14

The title of our first poem, "Just for Fun," begins the attack on the hunters who kill the green bird for pleasure. The impulse toward balance that we all have, the instinct to shape things neatly, has given us "shades of green" to go with "shades of Red," and the balance, reinforced by the use of capital letters, of "BANG!" and "DEAD!" And something of the sense of the bird's long fall, and of the speaker's increasingly intense feelings about it, is reproduced in the poem's conclusion (lines 8-14).

But this poem is mostly a fake. (It breaks Rules 2.1, 2.2, 2.3, 2.6, 2.7, 2.9, and 2.10, if you are keeping score.) If the author's heart had been touched by the bird's death, we would read his report with interest, but this poem is not a report of an experience like that. It is an expression of opinion: "Those cruel hunters! They killed the pretty bird. I am terrifically sensitive and compassionate; the hunters are not. If you say you don't like my poem you are as bad as the hunters. If you say you do like it, you are a good person, although not as good as I am."

Author of "Just for Fun": I didn't say anything like that at all.
Me: No?

[7]

Author: No! I'm just telling how I feel. You don't have to feel the same way.

Me: Isn't your title an attack on the hunters, a kind of sneer at them?

Author: No! It means just what it says: the hunters do this "just for fun." I didn't mean to put in the sneer. The poem is about my feelings of compassion, not about any angry opinion of other people.

Me: You say you didn't intend to put in the sneer, but you did put it in. It's there. If you didn't put it in, who did?

Author: There is no sneer in it!

Me: Would you please read the poem out loud to us?

Author: All right. (He reads it. Read it yourself again, slowly, and listen to its tones. It might help to read it out loud, and always just as slowly as it will let you.)

Me: Thank you. We can all hear that it is a poem full of righteous anger and even more full of the proud display of its anger and righteousness. You sneer at anyone who doesn't think the same way you do about hunting.

Author: I do not!

Me: (Liar!)

Author: (Bastard!)

Me: This green-feathered bird, when it is flying free (line 1), is there a difference between flying free and just plain old flying? It does sound nice, "flying/free," those two f's, and that terrific word "free," but isn't it an attempt to make us like the bird rather than an attempt to help us *see* it? "Free" doesn't tell us how the bird looks in flight.

Author: It does, a little.

Me: It would be better if you used words that do what you want to do, a lot. It would help to let your readers see the bird as you saw it. But, of course, the real problem here is that you didn't see any bird at all. You *thought* about the idea of birds flying and being killed, but you didn't *see* them.

Author: Yes I did. I've seen hunters kill birds lots of times.

Me: The poem doesn't prove that you saw that even once. It is a remarkable bird you claim to have seen. It flies free until it, or you, can *see* the hunter's gun (line 2). Then it stops flying free and, I

[8]

guess, flies some other way. No wonder you mourn this bird's death: it is the most remarkable bird in the history of the universe. It flies away from the sight of a gun!

Author: I didn't mean that. It's just a way of speaking.

Me: Of course it is just a way of speaking, the way we all speak sometimes, with carelessness, a lack of precision, a halfhearted sort of accuracy. It is the way we speak when we don't care much about what we are speaking about. It is exactly the way of speaking we don't do when we write poems.

Author: Is it such a big deal?

Me: Yes, especially if you do it a lot—and you do it a lot. How high up does this bird fly?

Author: Very high. I don't know how many feet, but very high.

Me: When you look up at it, can you tell what color it is, or is it too high for that? It seems to take a rather long time to fall all the way to the ground. That's why I wonder about its altitude. It has to fly low enough for you to distinguish between the different shades of green on its feathers, and low enough for the bullets to reach it, yet high enough for its fall to take awhile. After it is shot, you speak of seeing shades of red. What is that "Red"? And why the capital letter?

Author: Blood, and the capital goes with the capital letters on BANG and DEAD.

Me: Good, neat, the capital R is a kind of raising your voice, for emphasis. It's anger more than sorrow that is being emphasized. And blood? Does blood flow from a wounded bird in several shades of the color red, so that someone seeing the bird fall could make out more than a blur of a single shade of red? Your poem keeps saying things about the bird that we readers can't believe. You don't believe them yourself.

Author: But people need to be told about the cruelty of hunting and about those endangered species. I want my children to be able to see as many birds as possible.

Me: Will everyone here who does *not* want their children to be able to see as many birds as possible, please raise your hand. Come on, just raise your hand if you don't care much about birds. (Time passes. No hands are raised.) Evidently no one here needs to be told what this poem is supposed to be telling them. And even if

[9]

there were someone here who preferred shooting birds to looking at them, would your poem change his mind?

Author: It might not change his mind, but everybody should stand up for what he believes. That's what I'm doing.

Me: What you just said sounds so American, so democratic, that I am afraid to question it. I would rather say that people who stand up for their opinions should make sure that the opinion is really one they care about a whole lot, and then, if they have to speak, they ought to speak very carefully, very fairly. They ought to try to convince others, not just annoy them, not just write for the praise of those who are already on their own side. Do you have a very deep interest in birds?

Author: Not really. I like them, and all, but I'm not planning to be a professional at it.

Me: That's what I thought. I bet you know people who shoot birds just for fun and that you really don't mind their doing that. They're friends of yours. That is the first problem with this poem. I hate to say it, but the best piece of the poem comes when you take something like delight in the bird's death.

Author: That's a horrid thing to say.

Me: I don't think it's a horrid thing to read or even a horrid thing for you to have done. We are not responsible for everything we feel. We can have feelings that go against our opinions. Read your poem, please, and listen carefully in your head. What's the best part of the poem? What word or words come closest to telling the truth about the bird? Where does your language sound true, sound like it came from your own experience, not from what other people have said? Read it and listen.

Author: "Fluttering, flashing" (line 10).

Me: Terrific. You have a good ear. Exactly—"flashing." A kind of thrilling, vivid beauty in that part of the poor bird's story. Your poem is most convincing when it sees the bird as the hunters do, when it shares their excitement at its fall. I hope you are not embarrassed or ashamed to learn this about yourself. The only thing to be ashamed of is writing a poem that is a fake—and I know you won't do that again.

Author: What should I do now?

Me: Write about something that matters to you, even if it

matters *only* to you. Write about what *you* want to, not what you think you are supposed to write about. Maybe you could tell about someone who is horrified to discover that part of him likes what another part of him hates. But leave the hunters alone. Your time and energy is too valuable to be spent in scolding them.

Expectations

Expect from life: nothing; let it overwhelm you with joy   1
   flowering your existence with blossoming beauty.   2
   Knowing that when winter arrives it will shy from view— 3
   to return or often not.   4
Expect from me: the world, and you will fall from my heart 5
   and I can only let you. For   6
Winter is the tragedy of life and great expectations the   7
   downfall of love.   8

This poem confuses the reader in so many ways it is difficult to know where to begin to complain. In line 5 the speaker—who I will call "her" for convenience—seems to be addressing a person—I will call that person "him"—who is her lover or suitor. Is line 1 also addressed to him, or is it said to the reader, which means any reader, which means everybody? And the last sentence? It cannot be said to "him." It sounds miles too big. It belongs on the stage or in a pulpit or in a movie: the old mystic of the Himalayas rewards Errol Flynn for crawling up the mountain, in the great blizzard, by whispering lines 7 and 8 to him. The sentence is not at all the language of intimacy; it is highfalutin. (It is what many of us call "bull.") Maybe the entire poem isn't said out loud at all. "She" is talking to herself, and as she does so she shifts her attention from life in general, to her boyfriend, and then back to the world of everybody. Is that it? Maybe. But if all we can say, after reading the poem carefully, is maybe, the writer has made us guess (see Rule 2.5).

If we think that at least some of the poem is directed to the world at large, I don't see how we can avoid the conclusion that the speaker is—forgive me—a pompous ass: pompous for her stilted language, an ass for speaking to me, and to you, as if she were the fount of all wisdom and we a bunch of numskulls cringing at her feet. And what about that wisdom she gives us? Is it true? True like 2 and 2 equals 4 is true, or true the way wisdom is true? I knew a girl once who discoverd to her great delight that her great expectations turned out to be the beginning of a great love. And all it takes is one case to refute a general principle. On the other hand, if the last sentence of "Expectations" was said by the "her" of the poem to the "him" after some heated argument or painful confrontation, it wouldn't be true absolutely, but it might be true to her feelings at that moment. But again, the last sentence of the poem doesn't sound as if any human being would actually say it to another one. No matter how hard I try, I can't find a way to get this poem to make clear sense to me. It tells me next to nothing about the speaker's character or history, or about the events that led up to the speech, or about the conditions under which it was made. I ask: Who is talking to whom, about what, where, when? And I get no reply.

The poem also confuses us because of its grammatical obscurities. In line 1, "it" is "life." What is "it" in line 3? There are several possibilities ("winter," "beauty," "existence," "life"), none clearly the best. What, exactly, does "shy from view" mean? Is there some point to the awkwardness of line 4? If you can confidently answer those questions, you are a mind reader.

Line 2 has what people who don't know better think poetry is all about: flowers and "existence." I know what it means to flour a baking pan, but how do you flower an "existence"? Come to think of it, what *is* an "existence"? I doubt that line 2 is the result of showing off, but I cannot believe either that the poem's author knows any better than I do what line 2 means. Perhaps the author thought she had to put the flowers in. She doesn't—and she hardly puts them in at all. One unnamed flower enters in line 2 and never appears again (unless winter, in line 7, reminds us of flowers). Line 2 explains, or tries to explain, what the experience of being overwhelmed with joy is like. By all means tell us all you can about the experiences you are talking about. But does line 2 make any clearer to us the experience of joy? Have you ever had an experience of joy that was like that flowering of line 2? Can you imagine a fellow human having an experience of joy like that? Do you know more about him and his experience because you have read line 2? If you answered these questions in the negative—and you have no other choice—line 2 doesn't do what it could have done. I think the poem would be better without line 2. Take it out and we wouldn't miss it. This does not mean that line 2 contributes nothing to the poem. Everything in a poem contributes to it. But if it contributes less than it confuses, consider removing it. You cannot afford to waste your precious time and space.

While I am pruning, let me present line 4 for candidacy. Does that line help? Isn't it enough to say that when winter comes disappointment follows? In line 3, difficult as it is to be sure, "shy from view" means something like disappear, fade away, shrink away from sight. It is another version of "fall from my heart" of line 5. Do we need line 4? If we remove it, should we remove line 6 too, and its rhythmic echo of line 4? Despite the fact that this poem doesn't tell us enough, we find that deleting large parts of it does not result in our knowing less. The more we look, the less we find.

In "Expectations" expecting from life is compared to expecting from "me." The two things are presented as similar and parallel; each might help explain the other. That's why if we remove line 4, we should consider removing line 6 too. There is a balance in the poem's structure that is worth something, and to lose that balance would be a real loss. But if you read the poem very carefully and try to figure out the ways expectations of life and expectations of her are indeed parallel cases, I think you will get a headache. You will get a headache because the author of the poem saved herself that trouble. We are not obliged to write a poem that its author left incomplete, self-contradictory, and confusing.

Line 5: "You will fall from my heart." I wish I had said that. Not in this poem, but in some poem that phrase would be grand, in a poem that had other things in it that helped us understand what the phrase means. The phrase suggests a lover retreating, pulling back, falling from an embrace, and at the same time the phrase means "you will be disappointed." The picture that lurks in the words helps the idea of disappointment, puts flesh on its bones. The phrase sounds good too. It *is* the way a saddened but finely considerate person might say it to her lover. I believe the phrase; that is, I believe it comes from the real or imagined experience of the author, comes directly from experience rather than from the record of other people's existence, comes from the author's life more than from her reading. The phrase in line 5 has the ring of authenticity and directs us to the author's experience. The last sentence of the poem directs us to books, and to bad books at that. The author has stumbled on to somebody else's language there, instead of insisting, to herself, on finding and making her own language. We need our own words to talk about our own experience.

Try a little experiment. Read "Expectations" out loud. Try to read it the way it is written; try to say the words the way the words themselves, and their context, vague as it is, want to be said. Listen to the sound of your own voice as you read.

Now try to read the last sentence of the poem with tenderness, gently, as to a stricken person. The words don't let you read them that way, do they? And read "you will fall from my heart" in the context of lines 5 and 6. The phrase *is* tender. Your ears tell you. If you try to read the lines any other way it won't work. Try to read it with anger, with sarcasm, with anything but tenderness, and you will find yourself laughing at the sounds you are making.

I suspect you are even more tired of this poem than I am, tired too of my floundering attempts to show that serious attempts to understand it are doomed to flounder. I have a hunch that where this poem went off the track badly, at the end, was right at the word "for." It means "because," but is a much less common word. Have you ever, in conversation of any sort, said "for" when you meant "because"? This entire poem is one side of a conversation. When the decision was made to say "for" instead of "because," the author, I bet, forgot that and reached for what she thought was the safety of a word that sounded "poetic," extraspecial, tried and true, fancy, and so on. For a second, she lost faith in herself, in her own experience and her own language. That gives us Rule 3: Never treat yourself without respect. I think you can see, without my writing them out, many of the regulations that flow from that rule. They are parallel to, or identical to, the regulations derived from Rule 2: Never treat your reader without respect.

[14]

Getting Started

Our next poem, "Parting," is a fine example of a rule that could be part of Rule 2 and/or Rule 3, but it is so important it gets a number all its own. Rule 4: Never be vague, or, be specific. "Just for Fun" and "Expectations" disobey it, but "Parting" sticks out its tongue at Rule 4.

Parting

Sometimes	1
Love blinds us	2
And leads us	3
Astray.	4
We must go	5
Our	6
Separate	7
Ways.	8
Perhaps—	9
Never to return.	10

If you say "Sometimes" to me, I want to ask which times, don't you? And who is this fellow "Love" who led the poor girl astray? Why did they have to part? Is there something more here than meets the eye? Charlie got fresh with Susan and poor Sue is now down in the dumps? If there is more to this poem than that little story, more that could be of interest to us, the author absolutely refuses to tell us about it. He probably thinks that poems are not supposed to be understood, that they are scenes lit by the faintest candlelight or moonlight, that we are not supposed to get more than the vaguest outline of the story. He thinks wrong if he thinks that. How can we care about people and events we know nothing about? We read with our eyes—our eyes and all our senses—wide open. We have every right to reject poems written with closed eyes or sealed lips.

The Masked Poet: I wouldn't be comfortable writing about my girl friend and telling the world about private things.
Me: If you don't want to tell us, at least don't tease us by

hinting at the facts you have decided not to reveal. You could change the names, or the place. Better still, write about the people you know best of all.

Masked: That's me and Mabel.

Me: Not at all. The people you know best and most completely are the people you make up. Nobody, not even you, knows himself perfectly; much less does he know his Mabel perfectly. But you know everything that is to be known about the people you invent. Of course, you make up these people from bits and pieces of yourself and Mabel and others. You don't have to put Mabel in the poem, but you have no poem if you don't put *somebody* in it. Go and try it again.

The speaker in "Parting" is not, at the moment, very happy. He ends his poem with a sixty-four-dollar sigh: "perrrrr-happps." Yet I have not heard anyone in this room sighing. The page before me is not stained with my tears. Either we are a very coldhearted bunch or the poem's sighing has not done its work. If only we knew, specifically, what the author was sighing about, we might sympathize with him. Rule 4: Be specific. And when you are specific, you will probably decide not to sigh in your own poem. You won't have to. You tell us the facts, and if the facts are worth a sigh, you can be sure that we will sigh. You stay cool, man. Let *us* decide; give us the freedom to decide for ourselves how sad a particular story is.

There are some words that usually indicate that we are entering the fog of vagueness: sometimes, somewhere (as in "over the rainbow"), ever, perhaps, never, maybe, and so on. Keeping away from these will help you keep on the good side of Rule 4.

Did you notice that "Parting" begins with four lines ending in "Astray," and then has four more lines that end in "Ways"? Another balanced construction, this time reinforced by rhyme. That's part of the reason this poem sounds better than it is.

Deep Thinker in the Back of the Room, thinking: (Aha! I will obey all these rules and make sure to put in plenty of balance. Gotcha!)

[16]

Getting Started

Me, via mental telepathy: (It won't work. Balance, form, the musical qualities that we have seen in our first poems, get into the poem while the writer is occupied with other things. Write a good poem and these formal excellences will appear in it as if by magic, free. The process does not work the other way around. If you think about how to write a good poem, you will write a bad one. Save all your thinking for the people and places and things in your poem.)

Pop

Methodically he starts with a base	1
of paper,	2
Then, some wood shavings,	3
And, lastly,	4
Four, split (not sawed) logs	5
carefully placed.	6
A faint odor of sulfur	7
Irritates the nostrils,	8
A ray emerges—elusive as the firefly's glow—	9
His cheeks work like broken bellows;	10
The firefly is gone.	11
He pursues his eternal flame—yet,	12
Unlike the Olympian,	13
He raises his torch again and again;	14
Bellows forgotten, he adjusts the updraft.	15
The flames begin to dart, snakelike,	16
Through the logs;	17
He waits,	18
anticipation lighting his eyes.	19
The flames grow,	20
dancing abandonedly in their frenzy;	21
He whirls, and extinguishing all other light,	22
Shouts into the next room:	23
"Honey, bring the popcorn popper!"	24

[17]

How to Write a Poem

"Pop" is a cheat and a fraud. I'm glad you dislike it too. As we read it, suspense builds. We are tricked into thinking the poem is worth our attention. When we come to the end, we realize that we have been had. The author—a twit if there ever was one—takes advantage of our generous interest in our fellow creatures, then laughs in our face when we learn that he has tricked us. The author's energy is devoted to playing this trick on us. He has no interest in the fire he so carefully describes, no interest in its builder. Pop is methodical, carefully painstaking; he's a man who does things thoroughly, without half measures or compromise. He goes to the trouble of splitting his logs—the saw (line 5) is easier, but it does not produce the perfect fuel he insists on. He endures irritation, exertion, and frustration. He is compared to the torchbearer who carries the sacred flame of the Olympics. We expect a lot from this man, expect to learn how he faces some problem or event of much more consequence than the fire for the popcorn. Or we expect to learn something worthwhile about his character from watching him build his fire. There is even a hint that Pop will come to grief: his cheeks work like a "broken bellows" (line 10). The description is rather vague. Just how a bellows behaves when it is broken I do not know, but the word "broken" has been associated with Pop, an ominous suggestion.

Then the author lets the cat out of the bag. Pop is no more than some pleasant slob in a television commercial. (Why he turns out the lights [line 22] before calling for the popper is a hard question. I bet it is for no other reason than to continue to fool the reader into thinking that this poem will be more dramatic, more impor- tant, than it is.) All his preparation, and that of his author, has been done in pursuit of trivial ends.

But before we consign "Pop" to the flames of damnation, let us remember the principle that nobody is as bad, or as hopeless, as the hopelessly bad poem that he is capable of writing. It is quite obvious that "Pop," however misguided in intention, was written with care, patience, perception, intelligence, sensitivity, and skill— good things all. Suppose its author had ended his poem at the end of line 19. Read the poem again, please, as if its last stanza had never existed.

See? Not quite a good poem, but in no way a fraud. Pop has his author's sympathy and the reader's interest. The fire he has labored over, and his controlled anticipation of success, come together at the end to light up his eyes and ours. It is a poem about struggle and triumph. The author tells us about Pop's fire with the sort of concern usually reserved for endeavors of much greater importance. The "Olympian" Pop is compared with cannot help but put into our minds the heroic exploits of Greek legend. The odor of sulfur (line 7) that Pop withstands, and the snakelike wisps of flames (line 16), carry hints of traditional pictures of Hell and of the serpent of evil. Are we prepared to say that Pop's fire-building is presented to suggest, or to be a symbol for, the man's whole life of struggle and triumph. Not quite. But we can glimpse an imperfectly done poem hidden within the bad one actually written out on the page.

I will play mind reader to explain how all this could have happened. The author of "Pop" set out to write about a man, perhaps his father, perhaps a father he had imagined, in any case about a man he admired greatly, for whom he felt love. Very wisely, our author did not write: "Pop is a terrific guy. I like him...." He knew that his saying that directly would have little chance of convincing his readers or of expressing his own feelings in their passionate fullness. We would have no more than his opinion. So he gave Pop something to do, and he let us watch what he did and how it was described. From this we could draw our own conclusions about Pop and about the writer's feelings about him as they are demonstrated by the description. This perfectly reasonable strategy—I recommend it to you heartily—did not work well enough to please our author. He reread what he had written, the first 19 lines, and was disappointed to learn that his poem failed to do what he wanted it to do. It did not satisfactorily express his feelings toward Pop. It did not come out the way he had hoped it would.

This is a crucial moment for many writers. What do I do now, they wonder. One possibility is to do nothing. The feelings the poem expressed were not exactly what the writer expected them to be. They never are. But the poem may well be truer to the writer's feelings than his expectations were.

The author of "Pop" chose the not uncommon path of surrender. He gave up the attempt to express his feelings, but he wanted to save what he had already written. After all, it had been hard work to get as far as he had, and he had worked at it with very high hopes. He could not, at any cost, give up completely what he had made a large investment in. He could not face starting over again from scratch. He wanted so much to save what he had that he allowed himself to turn it into a trivial and insipid joke on his readers. In a sense, he took his frustration out on his readers. If he was to be disappointed in his poem, by God he would make sure everybody else would be disappointed too! And for all he knew, there would be readers who would enjoy his new ending, readers who expect so little from poems that they would be happy with the pathetic joke "Pop" gives them.

Our author might have found a more common, though equally bad alternative for salvaging his poem. He might have tried to force us to feel some distorted version of what he himself originally felt for Pop by taking advantage of our instinctive sympathies. Like this:

The flames grew,	20
danced abandonedly in their frenzy;	21
But as he whirled away to call us,	22
His poor old ticker gave out.	23
When we found him stretched out	24
On the hearth,	25
His body was cold	26
Except where the fire	27
Had kept his face warm.	28

Between television and movies, and all the people who have no other models of human conduct and so make their lives into imitations of what they see on their screens, this ending might be almost irresistible. Maudlin, trite, shocking, and not without some cleverness, it is the beginning of a best-seller. With this ending, the author *dares* us to reject his poem. What kind of beast would withhold sympathy for "us," the recently bereaved relatives of Pop? That word, "us," appears, as does that "poor old ticker," out of the blue at the last moment to prop up a sinking poem. Patriotism, it has been said, is the last refuge of the scoundrel. Writers in distress have been known to take refuge in it too, but they generally prefer the refuge of sentimentality, the display of sentiment in excess of what the situation calls for. Our author's purpose, the expression of his feelings about Pop, has not been served, but he hopes we will not notice this, so violently have our emotions been assaulted.

Author of "Pop"—repentant: But isn't that what poetry is supposed to do—move us?

Me: Yes, but it is not a question of quantity but of quality. Nothing could be easier than to move your audience strongly. It didn't take me two minutes to rewrite the ending of your poem. I had a fine teacher, in high school, who explained this matter to me so well that I have remembered his explanation to this day. With great glee, my teacher selected one student from the class and had him stand before us, his back against the blackboard. Another student was dispatched to the back of the room and was ordered to fire an imaginary submachine gun into the victim's midsection. Of course the point is that if the intensity of the emotion produced, the quantity of it, is the decisive factor, a mindless and meaningless act of violence is far better drama than Shakespeare's *King Lear.*

Author: What should I have done when I saw my poem wasn't going well?

Me: You probably would have figured it out for yourself if you had been fully aware that your poem was in trouble. Nothing you could tack on to a poor beginning would help much. Start again, from the very beginning. It might help if you told us more about your subject. We don't know, for instance, what Pop looks like. The more you tell us, the more we can know and the more we can care.

Author: What Pop looks like doesn't necessarily tell us anything about his character. You can't tell a book from its cover.

Me: What you just said forces me to tell you one of the secrets of poetry. It won't help you write better and I doubt if it will

[21]

make you a better reader. It may hurt. On second thought, I'd rather not.

Author: Must I beg you to tell me?

Me: Okay. Your poem isn't about Pop at all. It is about you, about your feelings toward Pop, about your feelings, period. In the process of looking at Pop and describing him, you tell us something about him and a whole lot about you. Whether you mean to or not, the more you tell us about him, the more you reveal yourself to us. And very often, what we learn about your feelings, you are learning too. You discover how you feel in the process of telling us about the book's cover. You may discover things, and reveal things about yourself, that make you uncomfortable. But the instant you take your eyes off Pop and think about yourself or about what your readers will think about you, your poem stops. That's the secret. The best parts of your poem come when you are so intent on Pop that you forget everything and everybody else. The truth about your feelings, and the sound of your words, and the form your poem takes, are by-products. They come for free, when you do your work of telling us about Pop's face, his hands, the color of his sweater, the smell of the andirons, the texture of the handles of the bellows, the snow falling outside his window.

Author: Thank you, sir.

Me: You're very welcome. (I must remember that if I want somebody to be as appreciative and courteous as this author of "Pop," I will get him only if I invent him.)

We can look now at the fifth poem in our collection of illustrations of how not to do it. I hope your spirits are in good repair and that you will persevere. Bad poems, dismal as it is to be surrounded by them, are easier to learn from. Would you like to try your hand at "Respect"?

Respect

Yesterday in this beautiful land	1
People had "respect" for their fellowman.	2
They were happy but poor indeed	3
Although they worked hard for the things of need.	4

Today, this country is turned inside out	5
Half the people do not know what it's all about.	6
The streets are so filled with crime today	7
We're not safe at home, nor away.	8
There is too little love, true friends are few	9
What is this world coming to?	10
Time, alone, will tell if this nation	11
Can be, again, "Wonderful America,	12
God's Creation."	13

You: It rhymes.

Me: Yes indeed. Does that help? Isn't it an awfully silly poem?

You: She means well. Some people would find what she says interesting and worth saying.

Me: That's a terrible thing to say about "some people." I think this is a poem not even its mother could love.

You: The author is not a very good historian. She sighs well . . .

Me: Often.

You: I would prefer it if she would tell us why she feels so sorry for herself.

Me: Rule 4.

You: "Be specific." She might tell us about the "true" friend who disappointed her. What, exactly, did he do to her?

Enter, *Author of "Respect":* Good afternoon.

You and Me: Good afternoon, *sir.*

Author: I like my poem. My friends like my poem. I have lots of friends, a good wife, and seven children. I am the assistant manager for Sears, Roebuck. Nobody thinks I'm silly.

Me: The poem is silly, not you.

Author: The poem is just fine. It rhymes every time. It tells the truth about the country I love.

Me: You say, at the end, that we will only know what the future will be like when that future time comes.

Author: Isn't that true?

Me: Too true, alas. (Dope!) Seven children! How old are they?

Author: The oldest is nineteen. She's at college.

Me: Really! You're in terrific shape for your age. Where does she go to college?

Author: She had been at Cornell, but now she's living at home and going to the university right here in Akron.

Me: Yeah, it *is* very expensive to send them out of town.

Author: It wasn't the money. Mary hadn't been away from home before. Guess the girl wasn't ready for all that freedom, and being on her own.

Me: Pretty girl, I'll bet.

Author: Too pretty for her own good! Why a nice girl like my Mary would take up with one of those long-haired creeps—to look at him you'd never believe his parents could afford to send him to a fancy college. He went to Canada when he thought they'd draft him. Walks around with a damn Canadian flag on his back and an American flag on the seat of his pants!

Me: Spoiled brat!

Author: Slob! I threw him out. He ran his dolled-up truck onto my lawn and marched in to get Mary's summer clothes. She wasn't even going to come in out of the truck. Florida! And she came running in, worried about *him!*

You: (Tell him to write a poem about that.)

Me: (*You* tell him! Or tell him that he already did! I made him appear and I will make him disappear.) Poor.

You: He wrote that poem to make himself feel better. In the poem he gets even without anyone knowing what happened.

Me: He even gets his lawn in, with the tracks from that truck: "beautiful land . . . / . . . God's Creation." His poem starts and finishes with his lawn.

You: I think this case is hopeless. This guy doesn't want to know about poetry. His way makes him happy. His friends don't know, or can't tell him, how bad his poem is.

Me: Our only hope is that he knows enough himself about what he's doing to make him a little uneasy about it. He must have some suspicion that he's not perfect and that his daughter and her creep are not perfectly wrong. He's probably never read a good poem in his life, or even read a decent novel, so he doesn't know any alternative. He doesn't know what it means to think. His thinking is like a child's; he can attack and he can defend, but that's all. Reason has no place in his life. He knows that the people who say they like his poem don't know any more about poetry than he does. He can't imagine there being anyone who is smarter or better than he is. But I see some signs that even he is not hopeless.

You: You do?

Me: He came all the way over here to eavesdrop on us. He heard us talking about his poem, and he still came right in the door. And he *did* obey Rule 1. He wrote a poem. Some people get their revenge with deadlier instruments than pencils.

The Same Man?

His presence is unmistakable; his arrival announced;	1
Placed "higher" than others in the room	2
His garb, a throwback to a simpler time,	3
Symbolizes the respect we have been taught to show.	4
He is one of us—outside the room: smoking a cigar,	5
laughing;	6
Minutes later, approachable only through formality,	7
He listens—two parties vying for his sympathy—	8
Only one will win.	9
An interpreter of justice—a job like any other	10
With decisions as the result;	11
And later, again, outside the room,	12
Cigar in mouth, laughing—	13
Is he the same man?	14

The author of "The Same Man?" has discovered that people behave differently when on the job than they do when at leisure. One would think that by the time they reached the age of six or eight, all human beings would have learned this. But thousands of sociologists earn their daily bread by announcing that 2 is the sum of 1 and 1, and our author also seeks to earn something for telling us what we have long known. His discovery, like the discovery of all obvious truths, is not very exciting. It is very rare for us to be deeply moved by an idea. In fact, a famous philosopher says that the slightest sensation, like a mosquito bite, affects us more strongly than does the mightiest idea, like the curvature of space. And one kick to a deep thinker's shin is sure to draw his attention away from whatever large idea he has been contemplating.

Our author does what he can to pump up his own enthusiasm, and ours, for his idea. He holds our attention by casting his poem into the form of a riddle. He never does name his subject's occupation, as if he senses that to say, bluntly, "judge," would take the air out of his balloon. He teases us by "higher" in line 2. He knows that his man is a judge and that his courtroom seat is elevated, but if he simply told us that right off, in plain English, we would see that this poem has very little to tell us. The riddle part of the poem has nothing whatever to do with the poem's idea, but writers will do anything at all in order to hold their reader's interest. Readers with a modicum of self-respect have every right to be offended by such treatment. They are under no obligation to continue reading.

Having set up his riddle, the author now tries to delay as long as he can our finding the solution to it. The longer it takes us, the longer we are at his mercy. So he resorts to padding, to words that take up space and time, and do little else worth doing. Lines 8, 9, and 10 are padding. So are the words "in the room" (line 2) and "the room" (line 12). In fact, almost everything in the poem that is not deliberate obfuscation is padding. (Obfuscation is action that darkens, confuses, or misleads.) The author of this poem is an inconsiderate trifler with my time and patience.

A rhetorical question, such as "Is he the same man?" is one we are not supposed to answer. Our author would be too embarrassed to say: "It is fascinating that this pleasant chap is also a judge." It is not in the least fascinating. So the author puts it in the form of a question. He pretends to have been struck dumb with amazement: "Is he the same man?" Of course he is the same man, you sniggering dolt.

This poem is about an idea; good poems are about experiences. We want to know what happened, not what anybody thought about it. Someone, even this author, might have had, or imagined, an experience that moved him deeply, and which had to do with a

[26]

judge's behavior in and out of his court. But this poem is not about a particular experience, or even about a particular judge. It is about *all* judges, about all cases of occupational roles. Unlike ideas, experiences happen to individual people in individual places. They happen at specific times. Experiences are always singular. In other words, author of "The Same Man?," obey Rule 4: Never be vague. The torments you are now undergoing are your punishment for disobeying that rule, as well as Rules 2 and 3. Go back to Rule 1.

Searching

I am searching	1
For the oneness deep within me,	2
Revolving around and around—going nowhere.	3
I think I'm at last living my dream	4
But discover it's a cheap imitation.	5
I've blocked out the bad times,	6
And distorted the good moments to happy fantasies.	7
I long to be wanted	8
So I destroy others,	9
Only to have deceived myself.	10

"Searching" is a fine example of what happens when a writer fails to tell his reader the detailed and specific truth of his particular experience, but it is not as an illustration of that problem that I have included it, and included it last, in our survey of misguided first attempts. The author of "Searching," like many of our language's more accomplished contemporary poets, seeks to use poetry as the vehicle for intimate revelation and confession of her most private self. This is based on the belief that what we would not dare to say out loud, or in any other forum, what we would even hesitate to listen to, may get itself said and heard, without embarrassment or impropriety, in a poem. The sincerity of the present attempt is beyond question. Let me ask you to read "Searching" as skillfully as you can. Read it as slowly as possible, just fast enough to avoid making it sound ridiculous. You want to let every word, and every bit of punctuation, register its maximum impact. (In case you wondered, as many people do, when a line ends and there is no punctuation there, the pause should be no longer than it takes you to carry your eye over to the start of the next line—an almost imperceptible hesitation. Even if there is no punctuation at the end of a line, there may be some grammatical reason that allows or requires a longer pause. Lines 4 and 8 end without punctuation but fall at the end of the first part of a compound sentence. The sense [the meaning, that is] calls for a pause, but a shorter pause than would have been indicated if the author had elected to use commas. By use of punctuation the author can control the pace of the lines, the emphasis and grammar of his sentences, and their meaning.) The point in reading is: squeeze as much out of the poem as you can. And you must not only squeeze, you must listen to how it sounds as it comes out of your mouth. The "playing time" for "Searching" that feels right to me is just a tad less than thirty seconds.

How would you describe how this poem sounds to your ear? I said its tone, its voice, was sincere. It is also, despite the poem's emotionally intense subject, calm and controlled. The speaker's self-control, which we can hear, leaves its mark on the poem in visible ways too. The ten-line poem is broken into two stanzas of equal length. Each stanza contains two sentences, each one beginning with the word "I." Each stanza moves toward a reversal that the last sentences of each announce with their opening words: "But" (line 5) and "Only" (line 10). Each stanza, and the entire poem, moves toward the climactic discovery of self-deception. That discovery is announced in line 5, and announced again, with increased bite and finality, by line 10.

All this raises an important and disconcerting question: How can a confession of personal torment be both sincere and controlled, both spontaneous and not spontaneous? If the speaker in "Searching" is telling the truth, if she is really in the terrible quandary she describes, if she has in fact discovered to her horror that her life is "a cheap imitation" and that her loneliness has led her to "destroy others," why on earth is she not screaming or cutting her wrists or blubbering out her anguish in fragments of unformed and unbalanced speech? How can we believe that the

[28]

distress she describes to us is genuine when the only thing she does right before us, the only thing we *know* she does because we can see it and hear it, is to write this carefully controlled poem. The speaker says she is going "around and around—going nowhere," but the poem she writes goes with some precision toward a clearly stated and satisfactory conclusion.

"Searching" is in many ways a severely imperfect poem, but it illustrates a question raised by great masterpieces and by common experience: Why do we enjoy seeing a movie so sad that it makes us cry? Let me leave this question and another one with you: Why does the good feeling we have when we pack up our wet handkerchiefs and leave the theater (the glow of the aesthetic experience, I will call it) strike us as different from how we feel after seeing a newsreel or television report of a very sad event? A principle that arises from consideration of these questions is that life and art, although they seem similar or even identical, are not identical or equivalent to each other. In other words, your poems and your experiences are not interchangeable. Artists pretend they don't know this.

"Searching," to return to the earth, is too vague. We are not told enough about the specifics of the case. Isn't it vital to our understanding of the poem that we readers know, for example, the age of the speaker (the age, that is, of the invented character who speaks in the poem, not the age of the poem's author)? Is she a seventeen-year-old whose boyfriend has proved untrue, or a fifty-year-old survivor of complex marital relationships? (Is she, for that matter, a nun, an actress?) Poems are always about individual cases; the reader of this one is not allowed to know enough about the particular case set before him. What seemed like a confessional poem withholds much more than it confesses.

Not only are the words with which the speaker of "Searching" tells her tale vague, they are *not her own* words. The words of the English language are nobody's private property. They are useful to us all because we all use them. We build up our store of words from reading and listening to others, but we are not, ever, identical to any other person. What and how we feel about our own experience is unique, one of a kind. The feelings of other people, while different from yours, are often just a little different. When it

[29]

comes time to gather up some words to describe and express yourself, there are usually loads of words and phrases in your head that you have heard other people use, words and phrases that come close to fitting your own needs. There they are, neatly assembled, hanging comfortably within reach, yours for the taking: "the oneness deep within me," "revolving around and around," "going nowhere," "living my dream." But no matter how quickly and easily you could take such words, no matter how closely they approximate your needs, do not touch! Close is not good enough. You are a valuable addition to our planet's history exactly because you are not somebody else, however close. Somebody else's words will not do. At whatever cost, you must start from scratch and find and combine your own words, words that do not, even accidentally, remind you or us of some other persons. When words come to you after a period of intense concentration on your subject, you must make sure that your mind has not gone off on its own and saved itself trouble by plucking words off somebody else's tree while your back was turned. A word or phrase that is obviously not yours is called a cliché. Even if you are the only person who can tell that a word is not your own, do not use it. Rule 5: Do not use other people's words. Or: Find your own language.

Me: Are you still there?

You: Just barely.

Me: I don't blame you for being exhausted. Part of the trouble is that this subject does not lend itself to step-by-step treatment very readily.

You: The rules make sense.

Me: How nice of you to say so.

Rule 1 Write a poem, and keep writing them.

Rule 2 Treat your reader with respect.

Rule 3 Treat yourself with respect.

Rule 4 Be specific.

Rule 5 Find your own words.

But they are rules, not directions, and they broaden out into each other as if they were all part of one big rule. I guess the big rule is Rule 1, but that won't help much. Are you bewildered?

You: Perplexed.

Me: If you weren't I'd be worried about both of us. How did your poem stack up?

You: The next one will be better.

Me: I'm sure. Have you got a subject?

You: That's what I'm perplexed about most. I don't want to be trivial, and I want to tell the truth, but ... this can be a very embarrassing business.

Me: No doubt I misled you. I am, personally, very curious about other people's private affairs. I would like the power to float invisibly behind closed doors. Any envelope I find is likely to be steamed open. But this has nothing to do with poetry. Perhaps you noticed that when I talk about experience, I say, experiences that you have had or that you have imagined. What we make up, or imagine, is the best kind of experience for poetry. The stories we invent come out of our lived experience. Without experience behind us, we couldn't imagine anything.

You: Don't write about yourself?

Me: You couldn't write about yourself even if you wanted to, but whatever you write about, if it is a good poem, it will be about yourself.

You: Congratulations. Now I am completely confused.

Me: Good. We will return to Rule 1 in the next chapter.

CHAPTER THREE

Getting Unstuck

You say you are confused, perplexed. It all sounds fine until you start to do it, and then you get stuck. You can't find anything to write about. You say you need a subject. Tell you what I'm going to do. Lie down on that couch. Lean way back. Close your eyes. Relax. Where were you brought up?

You: Topeka.
Me: Where, what street?
You: 1726 Woodville Place. We moved there when I was eleven.
Me: Did you have your own bedroom there?
You: Yes.
Me: Did it have drapes?
You: Yes, I think so.
Me: Did it have a radiator in it?
You: (Pause.) I don't remember for sure.
Me: Did it have wallpaper?
You: Oh yes. Blue, with red figures on a gray background. Little soldiers, airplanes with fat wings.
Me: Next case!
You: You're done with me?

[32]

Me: Of course: The wallpaper is your subject. Describe it. Next! Lie right down on that couch, sir. Where do you come from?

Next Victim: Seattle.
Me: Brought up there?
Next: No, that would be Little Rock.
Me: Private house, apartment?
Next: Big old tumbledown house.
Me: Where was your room?
Next: In the back, third floor.
Me: Big windows?
Next: No, three, four, little ones.
Me: Could you see out of those windows from your bed?
Next: Not much. They were small and too high, but there was a round window near my desk.
Me: What could you see through it?
Next: The garage, the front of it, and a bit of the driveway. My brother would wax his car there, in his undershirt. I had to squint to see him through the sun bouncing up at me off the hood.
Me: Send in the next customer please! You can pay on the way out, sir. Yes Ma'am, just get yourself comfortable on the couch. Were you born here?

Ma'am: Oh, no. I lived in New York until George got transferred here.
Me: In an apartment, I guess. Do you recall what floor it was on?
Ma'am: We lived in one apartment on the tenth floor—10 A. I must have been eight or nine.
Me: Did you have your own bedroom?
Ma'am: Oh, no. There were five children. But I did have my own closet, out in the hall.
Me: Your own closet?
Ma'am: I wasn't allowed to close the door when I went in, but I could turn on the light by the long cord and look around at all my things. It always seemed empty. All those short skirts and dresses on hangers lined up on the bar meant for grown-ups' clothes. All that bare wall between floor and hems.

[33]

Me: What color was that wall?

Ma'am: (Silence.)

Me: Ma'am? Ma'am?

Ma'am: Oh, excuse me. It was pink or peach-colored, shiny, but there were squares of lighter color where boxes had been stacked against it. I'm trying to remember the odd smell there.

Me: Take your time, ma'am. I'll be right next door.

You: These subjects don't have plots. Nothing happens.

Me: I am just helping people find where to begin. Maybe what you call a plot will come along, maybe not. Just the remembering is an action, a plot. That can be enough. Try it. I'll even give you a working title: "Remembering the Wallpaper."

My couch is not always sure, and not often quite so quick and easy. It is not the only way to find subjects for poems. It is for people who are stuck.

The heart makes its attachments and has a long memory. What we remember—even if imperfectly remembered, confused, and supplemented by imagination—is what we love and what we are. Look no farther.

A poet needs a subject the way a bricklayer needs a brick. Do what *he* does: reach down and grab one, the first one that comes to hand. The less you think about it the better. Whatever your eye or ear or memory catches will do. Any fragment of your real or imagined experience will do. If you start with that you can't go wrong. If you have a good subject and get stuck, the problem is not with your subject. Don't let yourself use that as an excuse.

You: Could give us some examples of a good subject?

Me: I could describe some subjects that other people have used, but if I do, I tempt you to use a subject that does not come to you from your own experience.

You: Just as examples, please.

Me: How can I know what experiences have snagged on your heart? You are the best and only judge of that.

You: Ornery, ain't you!

Me: Your father's mustache!

You: Is that a good subject for a poem?

Me: There's no such thing as a good subject for a poem. There can only be good subjects for particular poets. Does your father have a mustache?

You: I'm an orphan.

Me: Did you know some older man who had a mustache?

You: No, but when I was a kid I used to think that a father was a man who had a mustache, used to think it was a kind of badge of identification.

Me: Where was this?

You: In the orphanage. There was a gardener there, with a great walrus mustache. I thought once that he was secretly my father.

Me: What did you do about it?

You: Nothing. From the window in the dorm, I could see him mowing the lawn. I used to think of him as mine.

Me: Was the sun shining that day? Early in the morning, was it?

You: As a matter of fact, it was late in the afternoon, and it had started to snow a little. But he kept on mowing, in the snow, and it was getting dark when I saw him. He had his pipe in his mouth, with the bowl down to keep the tobacco dry.

Me: And you want *me* to find a subject for you to write about!

Really Stuck: I'm still stuck!

Me: You are?

Stuck: I can find lots of thing in my memory, like these other people do, but what I find isn't interesting enough to write about.

Me: Is your subject dull before you write the poem or after you have written it?

Stuck: Before. I don't write about a dull subject.

Me: I think you are either lazy or scared. What was the last dull subject you had in mind?

Stuck: Elephants.

Me: All of them?

Stuck: I guess so.

Me: Pick *one!*

Stuck: Okay.

Me: Which one did you pick?

Stuck: The one whose tusks were used to make the keys of my piano.

Me: But you don't know anything at all about that particular elephant. Tell me about that piano. Where is it?

Stuck: Passaic, New Jersey. In the basement of my aunt's house.

Me: You used to go there to play it, did you?

Stuck: Yes, a few times a week for three or four years.

Me: Pick *one* of those times.

Stuck: I don't think I can. My memory isn't that good. Things from different times blur together.

Me: Good. Assemble the details you remember and put them together as if they all came from one particular visit to your aunt's house.

Stuck: That doesn't sound honest.

Me: You are not writing history or autobiography. We are not dealing in that kind of truth. You are using what you remember in order to *make* something, to make something *up.* The little boy at that piano is not exactly you. He is a character you create out of your store of remembered experience. Was it snowing that day in Passaic?

Stuck: I don't know.

Me: Yes, you do. If you want it to be snowing, it was snowing. A poem is no more a history than á painting is a photograph. Where does your poem, your invented visit to your aunt, begin? Standing in the snowstorm at your aunt's front door, or pulling off your galoshes in her foyer? Or was it a hot summer day? Was the basement much cooler than the street?

Stuck: I don't know.

Me: That's the one answer that make no sense. Pick a day. If you don't want to do that, pick two possibilities and decide by flipping a coin. What piece were you practicing that day? What kind of piano was it? What was sitting on top of it?

Stuck: An elephant! An elephant carved out of very dark wood, with real ivory for tusks.

Me: Aha! That must be the particular elephant we were looking for earlier. Was it right in front of your eyes when you were seated at the piano? Was there a light that cast its shadow on the piano, on the wall? Was it placed so that its eyes met yours straight on? Did it have a distinctive smell? Enough questions?

Stuck: I felt guilty about playing on the ivory keys that had come from an elephant like the little one in front of me. I felt afraid, in danger.

Me: Good. But don't write about the way you felt. Write about the weather and the light and the smell of that basement and the sounds there and the way the keys felt to your fingers. Write about the way the pedals and the keys looked to you then. The only way we could describe the way the boy felt is by describing what he saw, what came to him through his senses. You don't have to believe that; just act as if you did.

Stuck: Where should I start? At my aunt's door, going down the stairs, or just before I play the first chord? Which do you suppose would be best?

Me: Pick one, any one. Don't give it any thought at all. Just close your eyes, reach out, and grab the nearest place to start. If your poem doesn't turn out well it will not be because your subject wasn't a good one.

Stuck: But what if people don'tfind my subject interesting?

Me: People are not going to read your subject. They will read your poem. No subjects are interesting; poems are. And there is no way to guarantee that your poem will be good. If you want to find a subject that will guarantee a good poem you are fooling yourself. There is no way to avoid risk.

Stuck: I guess I am afraid of failure.

Me: Aren't we all! Even if no one but you will see your poem, there is risk involved in the writing. If you don't want to take any chances, you don't have to. No one *has* to be a poet. But don't blame your inability to find a subject for your refusal to take the risks of art.

Stuck: It isn't exactly that I am afraid of failure.

Me: Of course it isn't. We are all afraid of what our poems may tell us about ourselves. At any point in the process, writers can lose their courage and destroy their poems. They have many names for this. A few admit it was cowardice in the face of fear. Artists are not afraid of failure as much as they are afraid of success. Who can blame them?

CHAPTER FOUR

Getting Better

If you were stuck, you are now unstuck. You know the rules. Your poems are getting better, I'm sure. Pass that paper over here, please, the one on top. Yes, you, young lady. Thank you. I'll read it out loud as soon as your teeth stop chattering.

Pie

Mama always rubbed butter and flour	1
On the charred crust	2
Of the pies she left in too long.	3
The gray crust crumbled	4
Like moist slate filaments	5
On my fork;	6
Its creamy bitterness lingering	7
Beyond the syrupy rhubarb.	8

Me: I can understand why you're nervous about showing us that poem.

Young Lady: It's that bad?

Me: The only thing wrong about it is that you aren't at all sure if it's good or bad. Or are you?

Young Lady: I like it so much it hurts.

Me: Me too . . .

Getting Better

Young Lady: (Bastard!)

Me: (Sorry.) And I think you are uncomfortable because you think your poem is better than anything you've ever read and that your friends, the ones who like it and the ones who don't, will think you are some kind of freak. We live in a world where writing good poetry is not quite socially acceptable behavior.

You: Does everybody understand her poem? Do you?

Me: Let me try. It's an elegy. The speaker, speaking to herself, remembers her mother, or grandmother, or whoever stood in a mother's position to her, in complex ways and with complex emotions. Mama had been an imperfect person, an old-fashioned, bake-from-scratch woman who did not expect as much as she might have from herself or from her offspring. She knew how to make do under the pressure of limits. She patched up her mistakes, as if the patching really disguised them, which it didn't. The speaker had resented her for this, and for being given, and expected to accept, damaged goods. Now that Mama is gone, the speaker recalls her own feelings of disappointment, remembers with a touch of bitterness the coldness with which Mama treated her. She is disappointed too with the reserve, the distance, which were a part of her own feelings toward Mama. But the speaker comes to see, in the course of the poem, that it was precisely these disconcerting aspects of her relationship with Mama that are now most memorable, most important, most loved. The poem's action, or plot, is the speaker's discovery that her feelings are not what she, or anyone, would have expected. As is very often the case in good poems, this one has another subject too. It is a poem about other poems, poems that describe a child's feelings toward a parent in much warmer, sweeter, more simple, ways. This poem says those poems are wrong.

You: That's terrific! I knew that's what was going on in this poem, but how did you know how to put it into words like that?

Me: That's what I do for a living. It takes practice and confidence and nerve. I'm sure that this first run of mine at the poem is in need of correction. Try interpreting poems yourself; it's easier than it seems—just remember that you will probably make some serious mistakes. And it is very important to keep in mind that an interpretation is never more than an approximation. It seems so much easier to read interpretations than poems that you can forget that only the poem says perfectly what the poem means. And the poem is beautiful and lovely. The explanation isn't.

You: Aren't you going to ask her, the author, if your interpretation is correct?

Me: Well, I am curious about her opinion, but I have the poem before me in its completeness. I interpreted *it*, not her. The rest of you may be good judges of my interpretation, but the author herself is often too close to the poem to be its best judge. I do have a question for the author, though. Young Lady, what does rhubarb, in a pie, taste like? I've never had any. Is it stringy and very sweet, almost too sweet?

Young Lady: A little stringy, and sweet, but not too sweet, unless there's too much sugar in the pie, or the rhubarb wasn't fully grown. Don't you want to know about the real Mama?

Me: I know about the Mama in the poem. Isn't that the important thing here?

Young Lady: Look, I'm glad you like my poem, but I don't know where in the world you got all that stuff you said about it. I was raised by my mother, who is the Mama in the poem—and she is not dead.

Me: The speaker in your poem speaks of her as if she were dead. One does not speak about the living in those tones, with that finality. Evidently you imagine the speaker imagining her Mama dead.

Young Lady: The speaker of the poem is *me!*

Me: Not exactly. The most you could say is that the speaker of the poem is very close to some part of you at a particular moment. The poem sums up and expresses just an instant of your being, not all of it.

Young Lady: I'm not sure I understand that, but I want you to show me where in my poem you found all that about my—the speaker's—complex emotions. It *is* at least *my* poem, isn't it?

Me: You wrote it, no doubt. And you own the rights to it, I guess, but once you finish it and give it to the world, it's everybody's. Anyone who understands it owns it. I could say that it is one of *my* favorite poems. You wouldn't forbid me to think of it as mine, I'm sure.

Young Lady: You sure do like to argue! My poem is about baking. Would you please show me where you get all the other things you said?

Me: I'd be delighted to. Glad you asked. But first I want to suggest some improvements. Doing that may show you how I have read your poem. I think you should take out "always" in line 1. You don't mean every single time, without exception. You don't claim to know about every one of her overdone crusts. All you could know, and all you need to know, is that most of the time, regularly, habitually, she rubbed butter on her charred crusts. And your first sentence, without the word "always," does mean just that: regularly; "always" is a little extra push, the beginning of a sigh: "oooh, allll-waays." It is an attempt to make the poem moving by adding to it the irrelevant idea of infinity, an idea so deeply mysterious that it makes us gasp. The idea that Mama did it every time is not a part of what you have to say, not what you care about. It is smuggled into the poem with the little word "always." It is a sign of the author's momentary failure of nerve, a trace of her lack of confidence in the ability of the poem to matter to us on its own terms, without the help of the push: "always" is sentimental, an irrelevant expression of irrelevant emotion. In this case, the author recovers. The one slip is not the first of many steps on the downward path. But beware of little things like this "always"; a second step down is usually what happens. Recovery is rare.

Young Lady: Okay. I'll take out "always."

Me: I'm sure that's a good idea. Line 5 is not so easy a case. What is a slate filament? The crust was like those filaments on my fork, or the crust on my fork was like those filaments? Which is it?

Young Lady: The crust on my fork was like those filaments. The crust crumbled the way slate crumbles. The filaments are slivers, flakes, the sort of thing you have on a piecrust and on pieces of slate rock. They both fall apart easily.

Me: I see. There are no bits of rock on your fork. That's what I thought. The rocklike filaments are a way of describing the flakes

[41]

of piecrust. Would it be any clearer to do it another way? Like this:

> The gray crust
> Crumbled
> (moist slate filaments)
> On my fork.

or this:

> The gray crust crumbled,
> Moist slate filaments
> On my fork

or this:

> On my fork
> The gray crust
> Of moist slate filaments
> Crumbled.

or this:

> The gray crust,
> Moist slate filaments,
> Crumbled on my fork.

or this:

> The gray crust,
> Like moist slate filaments,
> Crumbled on my fork.

or this:

> The gray crust crumbled
> On my fork,
> Like moist slate filaments.

Young Lady: (He's insane!) Am I supposed to try all those combinations?

Me: Of course you are, and you already did. You said it the way you did, picked that one way out of all the possible combinations. It was done more quickly and less consciously the first time. Now we are trying again, more consciously, looking for something better. And I don't think we found any version that makes a great deal of difference. The problem, if there is one, may be "filaments." That means long, narrow, strands, as in wire. That's not the way piecrust or slate actually *is*. Close, but not precise.

Young Lady: How about "flakes"?

Me: "Like moist slate flakes." "Like moist slate flakes." "Like moist slate flakes."

Young Lady: Ugh! I hate it.

Me: Me too. Let me try to say why it's no good. "Moist slate flakes."

1. It sounds awkward, funny. "Slate" and "flakes" make a kind of rhyme that disturbs our ears, that gets in our way. The three words are also a tongue twister, hard to say even slowly. Nothing else in the poem is a tongue twister or has that kind of rhyme. We don't want this phrase to stick out, to call attention to itself and take attention away from Mama.

2. "Flakes" is dull. It's everybody's word for piecrust, and this is such a special crust.

3. But most important, if you give up "filaments" for "flakes," you lose the connection between the crust and the filling. The idea of a long string is in the rhubarb *and* in the filaments, and they both are part of a memory; they are themselves long strings of memory, reaching from the past into the present. That's what the poem is about.

4. Look how "filaments" fits the music of the poem. It picks up the *m* of "cru*m*bled" and "*m*oist," and helps say, subtly, "m-m-m-m" as in delicious. And "filaments" echoes the *l* in "crumb*l*ed" and "s*l*ate." It sweetly glides into "fork": "*f*ilaments/On my *f*ork." The word "filaments" conveys something of the lightness and delicacy of the bit of crust. Oddly enough, "flakes" sounds heavier. Listen to the heaviness of the "fla" against the lightness of "fil."

[43]

Notice the way "fla" makes the mouth open wider and the throat resonate at a lower pitch.

"Filaments," despite its lightly tripping alternation of vowels and consonants, is not perfect, but there is a lot lost if you replace it with "flakes," and the danger of harming the music by rearranging the words can't be ignored.

Young Lady: So what should I do?

Me: For the time being, put a comma after "filaments." Later you can play around with improvements and refinements.

Young Lady: Play around with it? This is the hardest *work* I can think of!

Me: Yes, of course it is. Sometimes it comes easy, sometimes hard. (It's like love. Whatever the price, we pay it.) I have one more spot I want to scratch. What happens if you change "lingering"?

Its creamy bitterness lingers	7
Beyond the syrupy rhubarb.	8

or:

Its creamy bitterness lingered	7
Beyond the syrupy rhubarb.	8

Say the three versions over and listen. What do you think?

Young Lady: "Lingered" goes with "crumbled" and "rubbed."

Me: Yes, it does, but the point could be that the taste not only lasted long but that, unlike the rubbing and the crumbling, it is *still* lasting. "Lingers" means it is still around and that the speaker is completely aware of its continued presence. "Lingers" announces that the speaker knows that the poem is not about baking. That we *cannot* have. It is for *us*, the readers, to see that the poem is not about baking. The speaker is unaware of that, and she must be. Overuse of the "-ing" ending is often a beginner's bad habit, but in this specal case I vote for "lingering." Do you still want to insist that your poem is about baking?

Young Lady: No, I know it's about Mama.

Me: About the speaker's complicated feelings about the invented Mama.

Young Lady: Why complicated?

Me: Because "creamy bitterness" is complicated. The first word means "good"; the second means "bad." You force them together because that's the way the speaker's feelings are. And you do it again with "syrupy rhubarb": "syrupy" means sweet and smooth; "rhubarb" means tart, acidic, bitter, not smooth but fibrous, stringy. What a wonderful kind of pie you found! Rhubarb! The word used to mean "foreign" and "Russian." It fits Mama's peasant style, her knowledge of baking, her patching up, her frugality. Americans throw charred crusts into the garbage. But "rhubarb" is also very American. It means a fight, a heated argument. The word complements this poem's subject in all these ways! Amazing!

Young Lady: I didn't figure out all these things or put them in because they fit.

Me: If you didn't do it, who did? Isn't it *your* excellent ear that gave us "*rub*bed *but*ter," and "*char*red *cr*ust" and "*syru*py *rhu*barb," those beautiful and beautifully appropriate phrases? Wasn't it your perceptive eye that saw that the butter and flour make the charred crust look "gray"? Your eye that linked the gray crust to the flakes of slate? Do you see how the flakes of slate are a permanent version of, almost a monument to, the flakes of pastry that crumble away so easily?

Young Lady: I'm going to have to go home and think about all this. You spend more time talking about how I wrote the poem than it took me to write it. If I knew that it would take all this to write a poem I don't think I would have tried.

Me: And I didn't say all that could be said about your poem— not by a long shot. But none of this interpreting has anything to do with writing poems. It is about *reading* them.

Young Lady: It seems such a long, grueling process, this kind of reading.

Me: It is the only kind of reading there is. With just a little practice, you start to do it much faster, almost automatically. As quickly as you write your poems. What I have been doing, so slowly and step by step, is what our heads do in a flash. Much of the time you take writing your poem is spent reading over what you have written. So you have to get to be a good reader. But while you are actually writing your poem, you must *never* think about what you are doing.

Young Lady: What?

Me: Until you have completed it, never let yourself think about your poem, whether it is good or not, whether readers will like and understand it. While you are writing, you can't think at all, about anything. Try it. Put your pen in your hand and the point on the paper. Start writing, anything, a letter to a friend. Now keep on writing and think about something, anything.

Young Lady: I can't. The instant I start to think my pen stops writing.

Me: Everybody's pen. All you can do with your mind while you are writing is say the words that are coming out of your pen. But you can do one more thing. Before the pen starts to move, and whenever it stops, press your concentrated attention, in this case, on Mama. With all the force you can muster, bear down on her, and on her pie, there in that kitchen on that particular day, on that fragment of pie on your lips. This is hard to say, so I will keep trying. You must roll your whole self up into one tight ball, as small as possible, and transport yourself into the moment of the poem's action. Every part of your being becomes a great big eye, and ear, and even nose. You become all skin and taste buds. And you squeeze. Press, as in ex-press. And then the poem, the little wet lima bean between your fingers, squirts up and out into the air. Its force comes from your pressure; its direction is unpredictable.

The process I have been trying to describe has been called many things: meditation, composition, imagination, for instance. It is an intensified kind of paying attention. It is what people do under the pressure of love. It is an act of love and love's cause. The poet-lover loses his sense of his own personal identity, so thoroughly does he identify with his subject. He "becomes what he sings."

Young Lady: Sings?

Me: What comes out in words when you pay attention in this way comes out as music, with music's balance and shaped form, with music's rhythm, and with music's magically moving sound. (See? I got excited and three words in a row came out with an initial *m*.)

Young Lady: I pay attention to Mama and all this happens?

Me: Exactly. As it did in your poem.

Young Lady: What if it doesn't work?

Me: It always works! What fails is the quality and concentration of your attention. That's why you must never think about your poem when you are writing it. Every bit of attention you give to your poem and to the process of its creation is a bit of attention taken away from Mama. You have to give yourself to her, and there is nothing left over for yourself. It is not hard to do this; all it takes is faith and courage. You need faith in the process itself and the courage to let yourself go, to let your identity disappear into your subject. You cannot be afraid that the result will be embarrassing. It can be frightening to relinquish control over what comes out of you.

Young Lady: I've got to think about all this.

Me: You are, of course, welcome to do that. It won't help you write poems. What you should do is pretend that you believe every word I've said and go do it. You don't have to believe it; just act as if you do.

Did *you* do it? You, sir, over behind those two guys playing tick-tack-toe. Let's see your poem.

She

In a park, in winter,	1
Snow freezing around her,	2
She sits.	3
So tense that her insides	4
Are drawn back together and tightly knit,	5
a hunchback.	6
She hasn't smiled	7
So long that should she try	8

The corners of her mouth would rip   9
And drip blood.   10

She sits   11
Weeping   12
Over footprints found in flawless snow.   13

With sad eyes   14
She watches a squirrel   15
Scratching at the brown knit glove   16
With orange stitching   17
Beneath the ice.   18

In a park, in winter,   19
Snow freezing around her,   20
She sits.   21

It's good to be done with all that talk and get back to the real thing, and "She" is a real poem and it has a better poem in it struggling to get free. There are signs that the author's attention to the lady in the park relaxed here and there. Under the pressure of intense attention, there is no time or energy to waste, no time to waste on words that don't add anything. Everything that comes out of your pen should count. What should we take out of this poem? What isn't needed, doesn't count?

Sir: The words "in winter" (lines 1 and 19). The snow and ice tells us that it is winter. But I liked it.

Me: Because it is musical, and it is nice to repeat it at the end. I would not ask you to remove the entire last stanza simply because it is a repetition of the first stanza. Repeating the stanza can count, can add something we didn't have before. It gives us something of the speaker's reaction to his subject. The reaction is: I have nothing more to say, but I want to say it again; I want to pay attention to all this a little longer. If repeating the stanza does this, it may be worth its space. Think about that. What else would you consider removing?

Sir: Line 11. We already know she is sitting.

Me: Okay with me, but you could defend repeating "She sits" the same way I defended repeating the whole stanza. I think the decision about sitting is a hard one, and one that only you should make. Once I warn you about the waste that comes from relaxed attention, it's up to you to decide what is inattention and what is intensification of attention. What else might come out of your poem?

Sir: That's all.

Me: Really? Well, tell me something. I need to know if the lady is a hunchback or if that is only a description of the way she is sitting.

Sir: She's a hunchback, born that way.

Me: Oh, my! And that's why she's so sad. How disappointing. I'm afraid you have broken Rule 2.11: Do not take advantage of your reader's weakness: "I never saw a hunchback I didn't feel sorry for."

Sir: What's wrong with that? My poem expresses my sympathy for her.

Me: If I said that it was trivial, I guess you'd be shocked.

Sir: I *am* shocked. You give us a long speech about love, but now I shouldn't love a hunchback. Why not? What's trivial about it?

Me: You shouldn't love her, or ask us to love her, *because* she is a hunchback. That's not love, that's pity. Just as soon as your readers find out that she is disfigured, our instinctive sympathies for her overwhelm all other considerations. As she probably knows, her affliction gets in the way of other responses people might have to her, responses that are not limited by her accidental member- ship in the group of disfigured persons. Accidents are trivial and meaningless; membership in a group or class is trivial and meaning- less. Trivial, of course, by comparison with the person's individual uniqueness. Whether or not this way of the world should be or can be changed is a question I will leave alone. People once went to see the insane the way we go to the zoo. So maybe change is possible. But our question is a different one: how to write a poem. Being a hunchback is a trivial reason, at least in a poem, to pay attention to somebody. The feelings the affliction arouses are instinctive and irrepressible. Once you make her a hunchback, all other feelings are blotted out. Your readers have no freedom anymore; you have limited their responses to the lady, trivialized both her and the poem's speaker.

Sir: I didn't make her a hunchback. My aunt was born that way.

Me: You wrote a poem. The lady in the poem is a character, not your aunt. All people in poems are characters, not people. The author invents them and can do anything he wants to them. They are what he makes them. I wish you would "cure" this poor lady. Let her posture remind you of a hunchback, by all means, but gives us room to sympathize with her without being forced into it.

Sir: If my character is not a hunchback, why is she so sad? Don't I have to explain that?

Me: That's a very useful question for you to ask. Rule 2.6 might cover it: A poet is not a guidance counselor. The poet's job is to see and sense things that the rest of us missed, to share with us his experience, which is himself. But seeing is not the same as understanding or knowing. Even if you *knew* why the lady felt sad, you shouldn't write a poem in order to inform us of that reason. If you know what makes people feel the way they do, by all means tell the world about it, in a psychology book I guess. It will make you rich and famous. But the fact is that you don't know what makes people happy or sad. Nobody does. And you *know* that you don't know. I'll prove it to you. Is your aunt always sad? (What do I do if he says yes?)

Sir: No. Sometimes she seems happy and gay. We never know for sure what she'll be like when we see her.

Me: (Whew!) She is always a hunchback, but not always sad. I'll admit that we can have a vague idea, something like a good guess, about what our friends' moods will be in particular circumstances. But a guess is not a fact. You don't call people to assemble around you in order to tell them what you have guessed. I will bet you twenty-seven dollars that you can't always be sure what your aunt's mood is, even when she is sitting right in front of you.

Sir: I didn't take that bet, but I'll agree with you. I sometimes have a feeling that she enjoys being, or looking, down in the mouth.

Me: The only thing we know with enough sureness to tell other people about it is what we see and hear and touch and taste and smell. If, in your imagination, the lady is "Weeping," say so. If her eyes are "sad," tell us that too. Exactly how she feels beneath these external facts, and how you feel about her, leave alone. Tell your reader the facts, and if you do that well, the facts about feelings may get told too. But not directly, never directly.

I don't think you told us the facts well enough, or gave us enough of them. What is weeping? How do her eyes look? In line 14, "sad eyes" is less a description than a judgment, an opinion. It is a summary of the evidence, not the evidence itself. "Weeping" is a summary also, a generalization based on component facts that are not given. As if your character's weeping was no different from the weeping of any other person! Look more closely at your lady in the park. *See* her eyes, don't judge them. Listen to the sounds around her. Smell the air in that park. See everything as well as you see the glove in lines 16 and 17. And waste nothing.

Sir: If you give my poem back, I'll work on it some more.

Me: Take your time, sir. We'll be right here, waiting.

She
(version two)

Without stir, without sound,	1
The snow freezes around	2
A woman on a park bench.	3
She has drawn herself too tightly	4
Together, like a hunchback.	5
She looks as if to smile	6
Would rip the corners of her mouth.	7
Small eyes, mud-gray,	8
Trace through tears	9
The throbbing image	10
Of footprints found in flawless snow,	11
Trace a squirrel	12
Scratching at a brown knit glove	13
With orange stitching	14
Beneath the ice.	15

[51]

Me: That is wonderfully better, in many ways, don't you think?

Sir: I don't think it's done yet. Getting there, though.

Me: Do you think this improvement entailed any loss?

Sir: Yes, the new version seems to have less music.

Me: A different music surely. Subtler, harder, more intelligent. I love how you expanded the freezing snow (line1). Freezing is an invisible process, but you told us what you could about what it looks and sounds like. You made that rush of *s* sounds at the beginning; and the completion of the act of freezing is hinted at by the rhyme of "sound" and "around." The rhyme is the only one like it in the poem, but the rhythm of the stanza takes attention away from it. We don't stop at "around" but keep on reading past it, so the rhyme is not disruptive. And in the process of doing all this for the snow, you suggest a contrast *and* a similarity between it and the woman. The snow slowly hardens, dies, but at least the snow undergoes this without a whimper of complaint, without any consciousness of discomfort or pain. The woman's life is also freezing, turning into a death-in-life, but *with* tears and sobs of pain. (We get the sobs economically, subtly, from line 10's "throbbing." We whisper when we speak of a person's sobbing; we don't blurt out those things rudely. I do admire your speaker for the tactful way he tells us of the lady's sobbing.) At the end, she is like the clothing visible through the ice. In the first version both the lady and the glove were described with the same word, "knit" (lines 5 and 16). That was, perhaps, more obvious a pointing of the connection than we needed. We, I guess, are like the squirrel, scratching at those relics of a life that is frozen over.

I didn't say all this as well as your poem does. I only say it at all to show you something of what I see going on in your poem. It may help us all to have even an approximation of how we understand each other's poems.

Your description of the freezing snow brings the speaker's feelings to us too. He is sane, sensitive, poised, perceptive; and these qualities, added to his sympathy, enrich that sympathy greatly. They guarantee and validate the integrity of his feelings. And how tactful is your use of the hunchback idea! You don't hit your reader over the head with it, but it is all there in one little word: "too" (line 4). That is manly, that regret; the words themselves, "too tightly/Together" (lines 4-5), display a speaker who is doing something like what the woman is doing, holding himself together, keeping himself under control. The speaker's sympathy for the woman could not be shown in a more persuasive manner. In sum, this poem is not just good for a beginner, or good because you are working for me, but good without qualification.

Sir: When you talk like that I think you are about to drop a bomb on me. What disaster did I perpetrate this time?

Me: It's remarkable that someone could write the two poems, write so sensitively through most of the second version, and still have to ask where the disaster is. Don't you really know what needs fixing here?

Sir: Lines 6 and 7 are an improvement on the old lines 7 to 10, but there is some awkwardness there still. That's pretty much all I see wrong.

Me: I would try "tear" for "rip" in line 7; "rip" is left over from the original version in which it rhymed with "drip" (line 10), but this is not the obvious problem. You have fallen in love with your own words. They do sound good, even to me, but you like them so much you can't see how poorly some of them serve your poem. You're supposed to love the woman on the bench, not the sound of your own voice: "footprints found in flawless snow."

Sir: It is a rather silly line, now that I look at it. The snow isn't flawless if someone's walked through it; "found" is unnecessary and confusing. I wonder if I knew what it meant when I wrote it. I sure don't understand it now.

Me: What you say shows us the signs or symptoms of a bad line. Your own music had bewitched you, and so the line is silly in itself and confuses the whole poem. That glove in lines 13 and 14—how touchingly right that it is one glove and not a pair, that it is of dull but serviceable make yet with that colorful bit of "orange stitching." The glove says it all. That's the proof of a good work of art: any part of it can stand for, as well as contribute to, the whole. Those footprints, on the other hand, are as vague as they could be. We don't know anything at all about them, or how many or how deep they are. They are pure mystery. It is like a dull scene in a movie that the producer wanted to have great impact. He tells the musical director to bring in the violins and lay it on heavy. That's cheaper than rewriting the scene and reshooting it. But it doesn't work. I wonder if those footprints are those famous ones, the "footprints on the sands of time," literary footprints, not those the woman on the bench sees. Your speaker doesn't look at them; he thinks about them. Thinking! Ugh!

Sir: Back to the drawing board.

Me: Yes. One last revision of the weak spots. Have fun. I congratulate you in advance. See you later.

You: You told him that his poem was good, as if you really meant it. Not just good for a beginner?

Me: I did, and you're right. I left something out. But he'll figure it out for himself when he's ready.

You: Figure what out?

Me: It will come from Rule 6: Read other people's poems. I would have made that Rule 1 except reading is so much easier than writing that you might take it as an excuse for not writing. Sometimes I think that's what writers crave most of all, excuses to keep from writing. Unless they force themselves, trick themselves out of excuses and into the pain and torments of writing, they will do *anything* rather than write. How do *you* feel when the telephone rings in the middle of writing a poem? The truth, now.

You: I feel like a great weight has been suddenly lifted off my chest. Sometimes, when the phone isn't ringing, I just stare at it hoping it will.

Me: Good, maybe you are becoming a writer. It's really not so odd that people hate doing what they love. Don't those track stars and weight-lifters like what they do, even though we can see that they are inflicting great pain on themselves? Writing is a kind of confrontation with oneself. Defenseless, naked, afraid, alone—and it will all go away, and nobody will call you a coward, if only the phone would ring or your neighbor would come by to borrow a cup of sugar. Read other people's poems, but never do that in place of writing your own. Buy one or more of the collections of poetry listed at the back of this book. Read through them. When you find something you like, enjoy it and study it. Don't be at all uneasy if you don't like every poem by every famous poet in an anthology. Your inexperience may, at first, keep you from liking some good poems, but that same inexperience may also help you be a pretty good judge. It is inconceivable that there are as many first-rate poets alive today as the writers of criticism—and of book jackets—would have us believe. This is, after all, the great age of salesmanship. Reading the poems you find and like will help you a lot. (Now I need someone to argue with about that.)

Figment of My Imagination: I don't want to do that. If I read other people's poems, my own creativity will be endangered.

Me: We all await seeing the fruit of your creativity, but it is your efficiency I'm concerned about. If you were going into the automobile business, the first thing you would do is buy a Ford and learn what your competition is doing. It would be awfully wasteful to start from scratch, not to take advantage of what you could learn from your predecessors.

Figment of Mine: Who says I'm going into competition with other writers? I write for myself!

Me: Don't you plan to show your poems to the rest of us? Don't you care what we'll say?

Figment: I don't plan and I don't care. I write only for my own satisfaction; competition is irrelevant to self-realization.

Me: Well, in that case, by all means don't read any poems except your own. Are you planning to observe the conventions of grammar and spelling, or will your poems be written in a private language of your own unique creation? Those kind are rather difficult to read, although quite easy to write.

Fig: Go to Hell! (Exit.)

You: A hopeless case if ever there was one.

Me: Yes, if ever there was. He's going through what we used to call "a phase." It is not his creativity but his self-esteem that he is protecting. He may grow out of it. In the meantime he has found a fine way to *not* write. He puts his energies into thinking about himself as a writer. His theory of art makes it impossible for him to be an artist. First he will have to invent the wheel—and he can't let it be round.

You: Can we get back to the author of "She"? You said you had left something out.

Me: Yes. This is one I'd prefer to avoid, but I'll tell you. "She" is a good poem, and the author will make it better still. But no matter how well he revises it, and polishes it, it will still have a sad woman sitting alone on a bench in a deserted, snow-filled park.

You: What's wrong with that? That's what he saw.

Me: That is what he saw, or imagined, and what he chose to write about. The more he writes and reads, the less he will be happy with that choice. It's too easy. Once we have that scene, we pretty much know what's coming. The scene is a cliché, like the freckle-faced ten-year-old with his collie. The boy and the dog gaze toward the field his father is tilling. Put a thoughtful face on the boy—a stalk of wheat held in his teeth will do—and the rest comes automatically. "She" is subtler than that, but it is the kind of scene an experienced artist will choose not to use. It has been used so often it is used up. (There is an exception to this. An artist can deliberately use a cliché in order to defeat our expectations, to demonstrate the falsity of other works that make use of, and take advantage of, the cliché's automatic evocation of emotion.)

You: But what if the scene that comes to you is a cliché?

Me: Reject it.

You: How do you know if it is a cliché?

Me: Experience, and taste.

You: Where do you get "taste"?

Me: Experience.

CHAPTER FIVE

Leaving Things Out

A poem: when in doubt, leave it out.

They are your own words, lined up at attention on the paper under your pen. The ink shines. You shine too. Saying the words over, out loud and in your head, feels good. Now is the time to kill your darlings, to remove whatever can be removed. At first this may come hard. You will resist abandoning words that cost you so much effort and that sound better each time you read them. You may wonder whether your supply of words is large enough to allow you to throw any of them away. You may try to convince yourself—so much do you love your words, so much do you want to be finished with the writing of this poem—that your reader will need every word now in your poem, even words you yourself are not sure you need. Here is Rule 7: When in doubt, leave it out. Do not argue with this rule. Do not try to find exceptions to it. There are *no* exceptions to it. Instead of protecting what you have from the onslaught of this rule, search for occasions to put it to use. Here is a procedure to help you do this:

Copy a line of your poem on a separate sheet of paper. Below it, write this line again, but leave out its first word. Below that, write the original line again, but with its second word left out. And so forth. Like this:

1 (original)   Just like little kids bouncing a ball back and forth,

2	Like little kids bouncing a ball back and forth,
3	Just little kids bouncing a ball back and forth,
4	Just like kids bouncing a ball back and forth,
5	Just like little bouncing a ball back and forth,
6	Just like little kids a ball back and forth,
7	Just like little kids bouncing ball back and forth,
8	Just like little kids bouncing a back and forth,
9	Just like little kids bouncing a ball and forth,
10	Just like little kids bouncing a ball back forth,
11	Just like little kids bouncing a ball back and

Some of these versions of your original line are clearly absurd (versions 5, 6, 7, 8, 9, 11). Version 10 makes no sense as it stands but suggests the possibility of inserting a comma between "back" and "forth." Write version 10, with the new comma, on the next line.

Versions 9-11 suggest to me, perhaps to you also, the possibility of omitting the entire phrase, "back and forth." After all, that's how kids actually do bounce a ball. We know "back and forth" without your using the words. Write the line again, below, without the words "back and forth." (Perhaps you want the reader to know that the kids are bouncing the ball and forth *to each other*. Perhaps that is the important idea—because the kids had not played together in the past. If so, rewrite the line so that this idea is unmistakably in it.) Lines 2, 3, and 4 make sense as they are. Cross out line 5 through 11. You now have five alternate versions of your original line.

a	Like little kids bouncing a ball back and forth,
b	Just little kids bouncing a ball back and forth,
c	Just like kids bouncing a ball back and forth,
d	Just like little kids bouncing a ball back, forth,
e	Just like little kids bouncing a ball,

The shortest possible version of your line is now visible: "Kids bouncing a ball." Will that do? If so, that is your new line. Is something gone, something missing that you must not lose? Try again:

> Just like kids bouncing a ball,
> Like kids bouncing a ball,

I hope this tedious procedure has helped you see that there is no reason to tell us that kids are "little." If there is a reason to say more than "kids," "little" doesn't say it.

Is "Just" necessary? Does it mean "exactly"? Is the point that something else is exactly like the kids bouncing the ball, or is the resemblance no more than approximate? Unless you mean that the resemblance is very close, even exact, omit "Just." Why say something is exactly alike when you and everybody else know that it is merely roughly alike? Perhaps you want to emphasize the similarity? Perhaps the similarity is so striking to you that you want your readers to be struck by it too. Make the similarity exact and/or striking and your reader will be impressed with it. If it is remarkable, your reader will remark it. If it is exciting, your reader will be excited. But no amount of stamping your foot will make your reader react the way you want him to. Give your reader the remarkable facts; don't expect to save yourself trouble by telling him that the facts you know and he doesn't are remarkable. "Just" is not a fact; it is a sigh, a push. Don't sigh. Don't push.

"Just" may also mean "only," as in "He is just a vice-president," or "I'm just a little girl, Mister." In these cases—and bad writing is full of similar examples—"just" means: you must pay special attention here, give your heart to this otherwise unexceptional statement, quiver and go "oooooooohhhh." The word "just" supplies no other or better justification for its demand on us. It is, very often, no more than a whine of self-pity and self-indulgence. It implies that what it modifies is pathetic. It proclaims and celebrates a failure to explain, implies that a gush of sentiment is morally superior to a statement of fact.

I have made a mountain, but not as high a mountain as I could have made, out of a molehill. I hope it will make you very suspicious in the future of "just," and of words that function as it does in this example.

How to Write a Poem

Until you are confident of your ability to spot words that need leaving out, you should go through this procedure with every line of your poem. It will alert you to overlooked options. Do not forget the possibility that an entire line can be omitted. Assemble the new versions of your lines and read your new version of the poem. Try not to regret what you have lost. Try to like your new poem. It may need some touching up, some changes in punctuation, even some additions. You may discover that what you just took out has to go back again. Put it back. I hope you like what you have now. If you don't, it is not the fault of the process of pruning. Sometimes elimination of what can be eliminated results in a disappointing poem, a poem that seems less good than the original version. This is because the original's poverty had been disguised by extraneous materials. Be thankful that you discovered this. Let's try it again.

1 (original)	They have taken the life of my son.
2	Have taken the life of my son.
3	They taken the life of my son.
4	They have the life of my son.
5	They have taken life of my son.
6	They have taken the of my son.
7	They have taken the life my son.
8	They have taken the life of son.
9	They have taken the life of my.

Many interesting possibilities arise from reading these impossible versions:

a	They have taken my son.
b	They! my son!
c	My son!
d	They have taken the life, my son!
e	Taken! The life of my son!
f	Taken! My son!
g	They have taken the life of my . . . !

Leaving Things Out

h	They have taken life from my son.
i	They have taken him.

And there are many other possible variations. Which one of all the new versions is best for your poem? That will depend a great deal on the lines that surround the one we are working on. With the alternatives before you, it is a simple matter to play it by ear. Read the section of the poem, inserting alternative lines, until your ear says *yes, that one!* Your ear is usually right. One more example and we will be ready to play a game.

1 (original)	A small hard pebble inside the man's shoe
2	Small hard pebble inside the man's shoe
3	A hard pebble inside the man's shoe
4	A small pebble inside the man's shoe
5	A small hard inside the man's shoe
6	A small hard pebble the man's shoe
7	A small hard pebble inside man's shoe
8	A small hard pebble inside the shoe
9	A small pebble inside the man's

Although I do not have the context for this line, a version comes to me that is so clean and clear, so firmly sculptured, that I recommend it with almost complete confidence that it will fit: "A pebble in his shoe." That has the ring of authenticity, of achieved simplicity.

Now for our game. I will give you one million dollars for every word you find that can be left out. You will give me one million dollars for every unneeded word you miss. Neither of us is allowed to change the meaning of the original phrase or line. We will have to guess about its context. Ready? Here's one for practice:

He was a man of slight build

You: He was slight.
Me: Good, and good that we weren't playing for money. Now

[61]

for the real thing. This one counts: I want people to know the real me.

You: That's easy. I want people to know me. Two million dollars, please.

Me: You're done?

You: Yes.

Me: Good. Know me! That's two million dollars *you* owe *me*.

You: You can't do that. You changed the meaning of the original line.

Me: The meaning is the same. I made it more vivid, more forceful.

You: Probably too forceful for the poem it is a part of.

Me: Then that poem is probably very dull.

You: I want my money back!

Me: Sore loser!

Me: He crouched awkwardly on the sill.

You: He crouched on the sill. Crouching on a sill is awkward by definition.

Me: Unless "He" is a monkey.

You: (He'll say anything for money.)

Me: She slipped on the smooth marble floor.

You: She slipped on the marble floor. A marble floor *is* a smooth floor.

Me: She slipped on the marble.

You: No! You changed the flooring to an agate, a small glass sphere kids play with. That won't do.

Me: It would do very nicely if "she" is a rug. A rug could slip on a floor, but not on a glass marble.

You: (Expletive deleted.)

Me:

> The baby-food jars lie
> When they tell you of shining eyes, and dimples,
> As they sit in stacks and wink to remind you.

Take your time.

You:

Leaving Things Out

The baby-food jars lie.
They tell of shining eyes, and dimples,
As they sit in stacks and wink to remind you.

Me:

The baby-food jars lie.
They tell of shining eyes, and dimples,
Sit in stacks and wink to remind you.

You: Are you done?
Me: Not at all!

Their shining eyes, and dimples,
Lie.
Their stacked winkings remind you

You: Did you say "winkings"?ʼ
Me: Yes, "winkings"!
You: You left out the baby-food jars.
Me: No I didn't. They are there *twice* under the word "their."
You: But where are the words "baby-food jars"?
Me: If you are absolutely sure they are needed, you will find them somewhere in the poem. Probably in the title.

With nostrils flaring in anger.

You: With nostrils flaring.
Me: Nostrils flaring.

But I just had to do it.

You: But I had to do it.
Me: I had to do it.
You: I had to.
Me: Touché! What a nice example of making a statement stronger by eliminating half of it. What we took out was not the

[63]

assertion but the cowering, the whine, that had accompanied it. The original effort to make it stronger had weakened it. Try this:

No gas is readily available to him.

You: No gas is available.
Me: No gas! It is hard to imagine a context in which this shortest version would be incomplete or confusing. Here:

Periodic gusts of wind.

You: Gusts of wind. That's what gusts *are:* periodic.
Me: Congratulations. But it can be: Gusts. A gust is a gust of wind unless we are told otherwise. Try some easier ones.

Dotted with occasional weeds

You: Dotted with weeds. Dotted *means* occasional.
Me: It was brown in color.
You: It was brown.
Me: Brown. Try again.

In varying shades of gray.

You: In shades of gray.
Me: Your cries of passion haunt me still.
You: Your cries haunt me still.
Me: Your cries haunt me. Haunt means they don't go away, they are here, *still* here. Last chance to get your money back:

She seemed beautiful to me.

You: She seemed beautiful.
Me: Beautiful! Pay up.
You: Give me one more chance.
Me: Sure. Try this: "This has been a positive learning experience."
You: I'd omit the entire line, all of it.

Leaving Things Out

Me: Good for you. It is the language of the walking dead. You just saved yourself seven million dollars. Take me out to lunch and I'll call it even.

You: I am temporarily in a state of financial embarrassement.

Me: Flat broke?

You: Flat!

CHAPTER SIX

Stuck Again, a Hard Case

Troubled Soul: This is all very interesting, but when *I* start to write a poem nothing works. I understand what you are saying: I obey the rules, I try hard, and all I have to show for it is a basket of crumpled paper. I won't ask for my money back, but you *did* guarantee success.

Me: Many people are not actually stuck at this point. Sometimes the fragments crumpled and discarded contain better poems or bits of poems than pages other people are proud of having written. Perhaps your critical sense has outrun your creative abilities. That's what happens to most literary people. They learn that great poets do it so much better than they themselves could that they can't think of competing with them. Geniuses are reverent, but obstinate and pigheaded too. If you have decided that you know what the best poetry is and that you are incapable of writing it, if the attempt strikes you as absurd and laughable, there should be little regret. It is no mean feat to appreciate the best, no disgrace not to be Keats.

Troubled: Who's Keats?

Me: I see. You're just plain stuck. You may need special treatment.

Troubled: Right. Let me show you the only one I finished.

Night Scene

Treetops melted into the dark green sky	1
And the moon sprinkled its silver.dust	2

Stuck Again, a Hard Case

Over the asphalt highway.	3
The weight of the pack grew heavier with every step,	4
The shoulder of the road became icier	5
With each drop of crystal dew.	6
Ahead the rows of crackling pines	7
Formed a natural tunnel.	8
Back down the twisted highway,	9
A bear and her two cubs	10
Scampered through the underbrush.	11
Suddenly, a flash of light illuminated the scene,	12
Striking the traveler's back	13
And making his shadow long and bold.	14
He stumbled around to face it,	15
One arm guarding his eyes.	16
The whining rubber and churning metal	17
Frightened him.	18
They were noises foreign to this silent spot,	19
And, until they passed,	20
Were totally unfamiliar to him.	21
Finally, the friendly blow of the horn	22
Awoke him.	23
At last! a ride!	24

Troubled: I didn't want to trick anyone, but that's the only ending I could find.

Me: Some nice writing here: the treetops melting, the green sky, the traveller's arm held in front of his eyes, but I can see why you're not delighted with the poem. The last line isn't only a blunder; it is the symptom of a larger problem. And there are other symptoms: the cliché about the pack getting heavier with every step, for instance. If that's true, it's true only because you fancy it a marvelously convenient thing to say, a lucky and amazing accident. It cannot be true to your hitchhiker's experience. He is a man, not a scale. He, not this coincidentally exact correspondence between his steps and his burden, should be the poem's center of interest and awe. And then you repeat the cliché with each drop of "crystal dew" (line 6). (I guess that is a fancy word for sleet.) By the way, "Suddenly," "totally," and "finally"

[67]

(lines 12, 21, 22) don't work. They do not intensify anything, here, or in almost any other case. Put them on your list of taboo words. These and other things are symptoms of the larger problem: you don't tell us enough about the traveler for us to care about him, and you don't tell us because you don't know yourself. If you knew more about him, you would care more, and this, all by itself, would energize your writing. To a degree, this can work backward. By energizing the writing, we can come to care more, and know more about, the hitchhiker. Look what happens if I apply Rule 7: When in doubt, leave it out.

Night Scene
(revised)

Treetops melted into the dark green sky.	1
The moon sprinkled its silver dust over the asphalt.	2
His pack grew heavier, the road icier.	3
Ahead, in a tunnel of crackling pines,	4
A bear and two cubs	5
Scampered across the twisted highway	6
And into the brush.	7
Light struck,	8
Threw his shadow,	9
Long and bold,	10
Before him.	11
One arm guarding his eyes,	12
He stumbled around to face it.	13
Whining rubber, churning steel—	14
Alien noises here.	15
A horn woke him from his fear.	16
A ride!	17

Better?

Troubled: Yes, but far from good enough. It's not what I wanted.

Me: What I took out does not make it *less* interesting, but it still has the fatal weakness: you don't tell us more about your traveler, and you don't tell us more because you don't know more yourself.

Troubled: How can I? He was just somebody I saw out the window of my bus.

Me: Aha! I think this calls for a new rule. Rule 8: Do not write history. Or: Make it all up. History is what really happened; literature is always what the author invents.

Troubled: But Rule 2.1 says not to lie. How can I tell the truth and still make it all up?

Me: Think about it.

Troubled: Oh, the truth I'm supposed to tell isn't the same thing as . . .

Me: Historical truth?

Troubled: Yes, thank you. See, I do understand you, but I can't do it. I can remember things, but making them up doesn't happen. They don't come.

Me: You may be a special case. If you're willing to put in some extra time on it, and if you won't mind doing something that may seem silly to you, I can show you how to make it happen. But you must do exactly what I tell you to, without asking questions about it, or even thinking about questions to ask.

Troubled: Wait a minute. I think I've been through this before. (Is he, is this . . .? Is he going to proposition me?)

Me: (I think she's apprehensive about more than she thinks.) I promise you it is all perfectly legal, proper, and harmless.

Troubled: Well, you made it sound pretty terrible, but okay, I'll do it.

Me: Good. You will need some sheets of lined paper. My handy-dandy set of questions is printed at the back of this book, but since you are here now, I'll go through it with you. On the top of the first sheet write the word "Hero." A hero, in literature, is the central or most important character, not necessarily the good guy or the one who acts most heroically. The hero must be interesting, and every poem must have one. In some way or other, the hero must be better than we are, more sensitive, more courageous, more thoughtful, more something. To read the poem is to get to know him, and, since he is in some way our superior, to profit from our acquaintance with him. Since we have the "Night Scene" poem already started, we can try to use the traveler as our hero. Now, on the left side of your page, write these words under each other in a column, "Name," "Age," "Education."

Troubled: And fill in the blanks!

Me: Right! Name?

Troubled: Harry Hitchhiker.

Me: Don't be cute. Name?

Troubled: Harry . . . Truman! No. Harry . . . Smith.

Me: Smith is so common it's suspicious, as at the motel desk. Name?

Troubled: Harry . . . Armstrong?

Me: Brother of Jack?

Troubled: Harry Williams.

Me: Age?

Troubled: Around twenty.

Me: No approximations please. Age:

Troubled: Twenty-four. Does it really matter?

Me: It really matters. Education? How much, what schools, what subjects?

Troubled: Graduated from the University of Montana with a B.A. in . . . Business Administration, Marketing major.

Me: Good student?

Troubled: B average, or do you want it on a point scale, 3.1462?

Me: B will do. High school?

Troubled: Jefferson High School, academic diploma. And he went to Fairchild Elementary School where his average was S—for Satisfactory. What's next?

Me: Religious background and practice.

Troubled: He was brought up a Presbyterian, but he almost never goes to church, and he doesn't care about it one way or the other.

Me: Didn't his parents take him to church when he was a child?

Troubled: No. They don't care about it either.

Me: Place of birth?

Troubled: Detroit, Michigan.

Me: In the city itself, or one of the suburbs?

Troubled: In the city itself. (This is ridiculous.)

Me: Occupation?

Troubled: Unemployed.

Me: Has he been unemployed ever since graduation?

Troubled: He worked for a marketing company.

Me: What company? Where?

Troubled: American Marketing Company, Indianapolis, Indiana.

Me: When did he quit? Or was he fired?

Troubled: He didn't quit. He's on vacation.

Me: Okay, but you'll have to go back and change your answer to "Occupation." Income?

Troubled: Thirteen thousand dollars.

Me: Marital status and history?

Troubled: Single. Never married.

Me: Are you saying that because you are bored with this questionnaire, or is that how you think of Harry?

Troubled: Who?

Me: Harry Williams, B.A., University of Montana.

Troubled: Oh. He was engaged once, when he was in college.

Me: What happened?

Troubled: She changed her mind. They both changed their minds. I don't know!

Me: You know everything there is to know about him. You invented him. Does he still see the girl, or any others?

Troubled: She's married now, with two kids. He doesn't think of her at all. He dates—nothing serious.

Me: Ethnic background?

Troubled: Polish.

Me: With a name like Williams?

Troubled: English, Americn, WASP.

Me: Residence?

Troubled: Indianapolis, Indiana.

Me: House in the suburbs? Furnished room?

Troubled: Modern bachelor apartment, around the corner from his office. In the downtown area.

Me: Did he rent it furnished, or buy the furniture himself?

Troubled: He bought it all from the previous tenant, a friend from the office.

Me: What's his rent?

Troubled: Two hundred and twenty-five dollars a month, including utilities. This is ridiculous!

Me: Yes, it is. But you must forget that and think about Harry. *He's* not ridiculous. If he's not worth getting to know, how can you write a poem about him? And everything about him, even his rent, matters to him, and so, to you. Next question: automobile—year, make, style, color. Take your time.

Troubled: He drives a Mustang, two-door, red.

Me: Year?

Troubled: It's three years old.

Me: Year?

Troubled: The year was 1975. It was his graduation present.

Me: So he graduated three years ago at the age of twenty-one. That was 1975, and so your poem happens in 1978.

Troubled: Of course.

Me: Not of course. You could have your poem happen in 1878. Then we'd want to know what kind of horse Harry had. Hobbies?

Troubled: Parcheesi.

Me: Don't be cute! Hobbies?

Troubled: Skiing, hiking. Outdoor stuff. Camping, but he doesn't get to do it much anymore.

Me: Any other hobbies?

Troubled: No.

Me: No? Nothing else? Books, music, sports, movies?

Troubled: No, none of those. Just camping.

Me: Are you sure about that? The poem's hero doesn't have to be heroic, but he is the center of your poem and he has to hold the reader's interest. To be interesting, he has to have interests. It's not enough for a hero to do something; he has to think about what he does. He has to be aware of, or curious about, the meaning of what he sees and does. He has to have an inside as well as an outside. And only you can give him that. Does he read about camping?

Troubled: Yes, it's not quite a hobby, but he does read about ecology and camping, and living on your own in the woods. And he plays folk songs on the guitar.

[72]

Stuck Again, a Hard Case

Me: What kind of folk songs? Like John Denver?

Troubled: No, he hates that. He likes the old backwoods music he finds in books about pioneer times. I guess American history, early history, is what interests him.

Me: Good. Any other hobbies?

Troubled: Tropical fish.

Me: Really? Or are you getting bored again? Why not take a break now. This process of creation can be very tiring work. Come back tomorrow. Dont write anything more on your man Harry, but think about him and bring your hero sheet back with you.

Me: (It is not tiring work at all, but this girl is resisting the process. She is thinking about somebody she knows and using him for Harry. There is nothing wrong with this—all our creations are based on what we know—but she seems determined not to think about her character, or at least not to tell anyone how she thinks about him.)

Me: (The next day.) Glad to see you again! Not everybody comes back.

Troubled: Oh, I wouldn't do that. (It was close, though).) I was serious about those tropical fish. He had them as a boy, and in college. He likes to turn out all the lights in his apartment, except for the one on the tank, and look at them. He even talks to them. He's got the big tank right in the middle of his living room, in front of the sofa instead of a coffee table.

Me: Terrific. Ordinarily I'd say you'd found the center of your poem here, but since you've started with the hitchhiking episode, let's stick with that. You can write "Watching the Fish" some other time. By the way, who's going to feed the fish while Harry's on vacation?

Troubled: I *had* thought of that. He has some kind of machine with a timer that drops food into the tank.

Me: I've never seen one of those. Did he buy it, or . . .

Troubled: He made it himself, his own invention.

Me: Very interesting. Is he what we'd call an animal lover?

Troubled: No, he's just careful, and patient. And clever. He'd like to be an inventor, and an engineer maybe.

Me: Good; now we need to know, and to write down on the "Hero" sheet, what he looks like: facial features, hair, eyes, nose, and so on. And his physique, height, weight, build.

Troubled: Blond hair, shag cut; light blue eyes, straight strong features, nice smile, clean-shaven. And he's 5'11", 180 pounds, muscular legs and shoulders.

Me: From all that hiking, I bet. I can see you are starting to take an interest in good old Harry. We are almost finished with him. What are his occupational aspirations?

Troubled: He doesn't dislike his job, and he would like to stick with marketing and get promoted. But he likes tinkering with things, and he misses the camping and hiking he used to do so often.

Me: What exactly does he do in his job?

Troubled: He writes questionnaires about dog food. His company runs surveys about what people think about things they buy. He does statistics and reports.

Me: And what are his occupational prospects? What's your guess about his future with the company?

Troubled: Oh, they like him, and he's very good at it.

Me: The next question about Harry asks for a summary statement of his personality. Is he a happy-go-lucky sort, a pessimist, a grouch, a go-getter?

Troubled: He looks like he's a happy-go-lucky guy, and everybody thinks he is ambitious about his job, but he's not so sure of himself as he seems. There's something sad about him; when he's alone, and not all smiles, he thinks about himself and . . .

Me: And about American history and the pioneers?

Troubled: Right! He is disappointed in the way the country is going, the way people are.

Me: Sure; he spends lots of time reading questionnaires about people's attitudes toward dog food.

Troubled: And about soap and deodorants. I think I'm ready to get back to my poem.

Me: Oh, no. Not yet. You have it all written down on your sheet. It won't go away. But we need to fill in some more sheets. If your hero has a wife or a lover, and if these relationships matter at all to what he is in the poem, you should do a hero sheet for her,

[74]

or for them. And if his parents, living or dead, are important to him, and especially if their stories are different from his own, we will want hero sheets, or partial sheets, on them too. In this case, I think none of those are needed. This seems to be a one-man poem. What do you think?

Troubled: I think we should know something about Harry's father. He's an engineer with Ford, a good job, but not a top executive. He's not like his son when it comes to camping or hiking. He was not happy when his son decided to go to college in Montana. They are friendly enough now, but there is some sense of separation between them. Harry is uncomfortable about that.

Me: Okay. That's fine. I understand why you want to get right to your poem. But you promised to try out my system, and we need another sheet. This one says "Place" at the top. The place where the poem happens, the highway or road where Harry is walking with his pack on his back. Why don't you fill in the "Place" sheet by yourself?

Place

Date: 1978. March 10.

Time: 5:00 P.M. The sun in setting. The moon is visible.

Weather: Cold, 20 degrees. Mixed sleet and hail just starting. Windy. In gusts.

Location: A two-lane paved road in the wilds of Wisconsin, miles from a city. Hilly terrain. The road winds through a heavily forested area.

Clothing: Hiking boots, dungarees, down jacket, knitted cap pulled down over his ears, Heavy backpack. Gloves; everything dark-colored.

Sounds: His own footsteps, the wind in the trees, the wind moving leaves and shrubs. His own breathing—then the car comes.

Smells: Clean, crisp air; a touch of pine scent. The wet wool of his cap; the leather of his gloves.

Troubled: How's that?
Me: Fine. In what direction is he walking?
Troubled: West.

Me: Into the sunset. And where is the wind and rain coming from—behind him, into his face, changing direction?

Troubled: Yes. the sun is going down in front of him. The wind is in his face.

Me: How long has he been walking? Where is he going?

Troubled: He's been hiking, off and on, all day. Only been on a road for an hour. He has no particular destination, just exploring. Going west. Can I go now?

Me: Not quite yet. Are there bears in Wisconsin in March? Don't bears sleep through the winter? I don't know about things like that, but you ought not to take liberties with common facts. Unless you want your reader to wonder if the poem takes place in the real world, or in a fantasy world. And the foliage. Are there leaves on trees in Wisconsin in March? If you know about these things, by all means use them. If you're not sure, try to avoid arguments. Maybe the trees and shrubs can be evergreens. And the bear. Could it be a deer, a fox? Or change the date and give up the cold weather so you can have the bear and more leaves. The point is: don't risk losing your reader's confidence for inconsequential reasons. Okay?

Troubled: Okay. Am I done with the preparation?

Me: Almost. The last part is the hardest. The questions that follow are important for you to ask yourself, but don't write any answers down. I don't want you to be too sure about your answers. The poem may answer some of them as it comes into existence. Here are the questions:

- Why is the hero in this place?
- What does he hope to find or accomplish here?
- What does being in this place mean to him?
- What is he about to learn?

Troubled: Why not answer these questions like the others?

Me: You invented Harry and know everything about him. But because you created him, he exists. To exist is to be free, free to surprise even you. Some people like to say that authors are like God: they create people who they do not entirely control. Writing is telling about your hero, but also it is your own way of finding out about him. After you have invented him, your job is to watch what he does, what he thinks and feels. If you have invented him well, he will teach you something about himself.

Troubled: This is going to be a very long poem.

Me: Why do you say that?

Troubled: Look at all the information I have about Harry and that road.

Me: That information is not for your reader; it is for *you*. It helped you invent Harry and his situation. Now we want your *poem*. If the reader only wanted information he could read the answers to the questionnaires.

Troubled: If I don't tell the reader about Harry's education, his folksinging, or his tropical fish, why did I go through all this preparation?

Me: I just told you. So you could invent Harry, come to know him, come to care about him. Not every part of the questionnaire is going to help you do that, but we can't know in advance what parts are the important ones. If you pay close attention to Harry on that road, close attention, mind you, a poem will happen. You will find out as you go along how much of the information you have will appear in the poem, but Harry himself will be in it. That's what matters. What Harry *is* counts. The details are trivial once we have him, but the only way to come to know him, to *have* him, is through details, masses of details. Information is secondary; action is secondary. You may want to keep in those bears or some other animals. You may want to keep that automobile. Or you may discover that these are unnecessary.

Now try to forget everything I have said about writing and concentrate on Harry. How does he feel, now, on that road at sunset? What is he thinking about? His fish, his father, his cold feet, his future, the people who buy dog food? What's going on inside him now? Look and see—and tell us. Go away and come back with your poem.

Night Scene
(second revision)

Above the setting sun	1
Pine trees greened the sky,	2
Shook and whirred overhead	3

And sprayed sprigs onto 4
The newly frosted highway. 5

It was good anyway— 6
The shoulder flat and wide, 7
Asphalt, gravel-sprinkled. 8
His footsteps echoed in the crisp air, 9
Grated like brushes on a drum. 10
The pack rode well, and, 11
At the road's high twist 12
He saw a clearing shine 13
In the mixed light of sun and moon. 14

The field was flooded, an early thaw, 15
And the rain came heavier. 16
He hammered in a tent peg with a stone— 17
And pulled it out with a finger tip! 18
If he were a bear, a cave would keep him, 19
If a bat, a shuddering tree. 20
"Racine 65," the road sign had blinked at him, 21
And he had winked back, 22
Sharing its secret: 23
He was *not* the first man here. 24
He carried the Mustang's keys, 25
Two credit cards, a checkbook, 26
And, from force of habit was it? 27
His pocket calculator. 28

He calculated that his feet were cold, 29
And would get colder, 30
That what he wanted most of all was 31
A mug of coffee and a hot bath. 32
He missed Walter Cronkite, 33
Worried about him more than the world. 34

He heard the wind rise, 35
Saw his shadow fly out down the road. 36
But the thunderclap that followed 37

Was a horn!	38
He wheeled round and hit his thumb	39
On a car's window,	40
Rolling down.	41

Me: Congratulations! You did it. *That* is a poem. If it were mine I'd get a new title, "Rolling Down." Are you pleased?

Troubled: Yes, but I am a little disappointed too. It isn't very exciting.

Me: That is the hardest kind of poem to write, the kind of poem beginners almost never write. It is a comic poem, a poem of good sense, not of passion. Harry knows that he is no pioneer, not the "first man here" (line 24). His calculator, like his metal Mustang, binds him to his modern life, and even that calculator tells him no more than that his feet are cold. Harry has a sense of humor, not a tragic sense of life. The tent peg that won't hold in the mud is funny. So is the remarkable coincidence that as soon as he gives up on the idea of being self-sufficient and raises his thumb for a ride, help is literally at his finger tip. Harry is honest enough to admit that his personal comforts matter more to him than does the pioneer life. He worries about the civilization he has left, but he knows that the familiar face of the TV newscaster concerns him more than do the important events of the day.

Perhaps this is what disappoints you, this lack of passionate conflict, but Harry is not the passionate sort. His heart was not broken by his college romance. He is not in rebellion against his father or his job or his country. He is a prudent and mature person, the sort you can tease, kindly, a bit, not someone whose fate makes for tragedy. He isn't interesting enough for that, and you were wise not to push him into a poem that wouldn't suit him. Or, in a sense, you could say that he isn't really the hero of your poem.

Troubled: If he's not the hero, the central character in the poem, who is?

Me: The only other person there is the speaker of the poem, and you could say that *he* is the poem's hero. The speaker's sense of humor is wider than Harry's, and it is the speaker's sensitive perceptions that give the poem what depth it has. Look at the first five lines. That's the speaker, not Harry, and the tone is not comic. The scene is set for a larger hero. And look at the lovely and suggestive fourteenth line. That's the speaker's voice too. The speaker's attitude toward the natural world is deeper than the man who actually goes camping. And the speaker, not Harry, has the best comic lines too (lines 29, 39-41). By comparison with the speaker of the poem, Harry is a dullard. It is the speaker who delights us, not Harry.

Troubled: I feel as if you tricked me.

Me: I feel as if *you* tricked *me!* But maybe it was my fault. I should have known that Harry was too bloodless, too levelheaded to be the hero of "Night Scene" as you first imagined it. If he had quit his job and gone off to the wilderness only to realize, painfully, that there was no paradise there either, if he had found himself at a crisis in his life, it would have been a different poem. Not necessarily better, but different, probably what you mean by more "exciting." Or suppose Harry had never left his apartment in Indianapolis and regretted not making his camping trip. You'd have to change your idea of Harry some and rewrite the "Place" questionnaire. We laugh at the first Harry, but we would not laugh so easily at a second one who knows beforehand and to his sorrow that he cannot recapture the supposed freedom of earlier days. Would you try it that way please? Once you see how it is done you can do up the questionnaire sheets quickly. Let's have a new Harry, one that moves us to deeper sympathy and greater respect. It would be very helpful to have you demonstrate how my system can work.

Troubled: Your wish is my command.

Scout

I would like to lie in the open	1
As I had, once. a Scout,	2
And wander through the cloudless dark	3
To the brightly twinkling stars.	4
To lie, head propped on knapsack,	5
The breeze drying my five-mile sweat,	6

| And hear no city sounds; | 7 |
| Only the silence of simplicity. | 8 |

Instead I lie on a mattress	9
And look into the summer night	10
From my air-conditioned fourteenth floor.	11
City lights fog the edges of my black.	12

Troubled: How's that?

Me: A valiant effort. It is not a particularly good poem, as I think you know: "the silence of simplicity" (Line 8) is, excuse me, abstract, pretentious, and silly. Line 11 is all padding, extraneous, as is much else. And there are patches of awkwardness of grammar and music in each stanza. And it's my fault! I broke the one rule that applies to me: do not suggest subjects for poems. Your heart is not with this Harry either, or the poem would have been much better. But, swimming against the tide, you came up with the "wander" of line 3 and that terrific last line. If anything could save this poem, that would be it. I wonder how well you would write if you could only find a subject, a Harry, you were personally sympathetic to, or could invent a Harry who seized your sympathetic imagination more forcefully. (She does feel deeply about some situations, but in the development of the profile of Harry Williams she was on guard to avoid situations like them. I suspect that Harry's story, as it developed on her page, came perilously close to her. She saw that and defused it. Was her ex-fiancé named Williams?)

Troubled: Should I try again? (I won't tell him, no matter what. Maybe when I'm older I can look back on Bill—I can hardly say his name now—look back and stay calm.)

Me: No, I don't think you should. Something is interfering with the process. Some conscious intention of yours, some personal anxiety is intruding on your imagination, thwarting that part of you that would speak without fear. We'd better leave it alone. (She thinks I'll find out, that my interpretation of her poem would expose her secret. The only real secrets, of course, are the ones that are unknown not only to me but to herself. But thinking about hiding her "secret" gives her an odd glamour. And there is pride

[81]

too in her desire to claim control over and responsibility for her imagination. She doesn't want to think that her imagination has a life of its own. The fact must be that she is afraid of her imagination, afraid of secrets that go deeper than the one she is conscious of. Foolish! As if there could be anything but freedom in knowing herself better.)

Troubled: Oh, I hate to admit defeat. What you're saying is that I lied about Harry.

Me: Maybe. You thought about a real person instead of letting your imagination invent the character *it* wanted to. I wouldn't worry about this at all. You're too smart, smart enough to outfox your imagination. Artists aren't smart that way; they have a childlike delight in their imaginations, but not much interest in thinking about what it is doing. (If she doesn't pick up on that challenge, I'll give up.)

Troubled: I think you're right. I was thinking of someone I knew, and then I deliberately made Harry different from him. Let me try again to invent a hero your way.

Me: Sure. Answer the questionnaires quickly, as spontaneously as you can; let your answers come to you without premeditation, out of the air. (And do not be afraid. There is nothing to be afraid of.) If you get a poem out of it, I'd like to see it.

Troubled: I will bring it tomorrow. (He's daring me to do it, as if I couldn't.)

Northern Woods Afternoon

From lip-burning brim to cool dregs	1
One cup marks the period of his visits	2
With the accuracy of the watch	3
I have abandoned.	4
Father and I sit above the river	5
Which, like our coffee,	6
Flows black, murmurous,	7
Flecked with frothy shimmers.	8
I distill my days into these seconds	9
Of slow talking with him.	10

As always, peeling Au Sable riverboats   11
Pass moccasin bends,   12
Fly-lines hiss in the crisp air,   13
Slap the quiet stream.   14
From their dark pools trout lunge,   15
Bursting in urgent spatterings   16
Of silver and brown.   17

We think of bait and bamboo,   18
Of hot sun on our necks,   19
Trout feasts, the cigar I winced at—   20
"Keeps the mosquitoes at bay," he would say,   21
And might say now if I cough.   22

Six miles away,   23
A river of steel and rubber and glass   24
Calls him back to the hectic grime.   25
I watch his car rattle over the bridge   26
And fade up the hill in dusty swirls.   27
I pitch the grounds into the water,   28
Shoulder my pack, and   29
Plunge into swampland   30
To find the fish of the past.   31

Me: That is a substantial and demanding piece of work. It requires careful and repeated readings, and it justifies them. I can see that it is about a boy who hasn't grown up, and he knows it, knows that he can and should. The father comes to visit, drives over from the city where he works, to see his grown son who is a sort of bum. Surprisingly, each man treats the other with sympathy and respect, and with patient regret. And the author, who lurks behind the younger man's voice, does likewise. A sad and beautiful poem.

Troubled: Thank you. I think so. I guess this is what I meant by "exciting," but that's the wrong word for this. The son wanted to keep or to recapture the pleasures of going fishing, as a boy, with his father. He seems to live in the very same countryside he played in as a boy. I don't know anyone who lives that way, and I didn't know I was interested in the general subject at all.

Me: It is one of the very few subjects that we are all interested in. It is what lies hidden in the disguises of everyday life. I guess Harry quit his job, if he ever had one. It's fascinating to see how his interest in tropical fish turned into this search for the trout, and how his desire for a mug of coffee reappears here, along with the camping gear. Do you see how the son's feelings get suggested by the details of the scene, by, for instance, the elaborated linkage of the coffee and the river (lines 6-8)? He feels a kind of sadness for his father, who has to work in the grimy city, whose son is a disappointment to him, and he says this almost directly. Most telling is the detail about his car that rattles over the bridge (line 26). Poor car, rattling from the hard use it gets, and from the ordeal of crossing over the bridge to visit and then to leave his son. That bridge is not entirely made of steel.

Troubled: The coffee and the river look alike. What else is there to it?

Me: They both have to do with the theme of the inexorable movement of time. The father stays only long enough to drink one cup of coffee; the river never stops flowing. The coffee and the river are what father and son share. For both of them the coffee, like the passage of time, gives pleasure, but pain too. It is either too hot and burns the lip, or it is too cool and bitter (line 1). Do you see how the act of fishing is a symbol that reinforces the poem's theme? Now's the time to show how smart you are.

Troubled: To fish is to pull something out of the flow of time, to retrieve and keep a bit of the beloved past.

Me: Bravo!

Troubled: I hadn't thought of that before.

Me: Of course you hadn't! If you had thought of it I doubt it would have gotten into the poem. It came spontaneously, from your imagination. Is a "moccasin bend" (line 12) a turning in the river, a bend as sharp as the snake's bend? I hope so.

Troubled: It is, but why do you hope so?

Me: My theory is that when you think about your hero with the proper intensity, your feelings toward him get expressed in the details of the surroundings you describe.

Troubled: The sharp bend in the river is a moment in the flow of time, a spot that is difficult to pass through, like the young

[84]

man's difficulty in moving on past his youth. It's a bottleneck. He's hung up at a turning point in his life.

Me: But the riverboats "always" (line 11) make it through. Your poem expresses a hope, a faith, that the son will too. Why do you suppose those riverboats are "peeling"?

Troubled: They are old, poorly maintained. It's not a very profitable business. Their owners don't paint them as often as they should. And water is constantly sprayed on them.

Me: Yes of course. The boats have to be true to the facts, but those facts were selected out of an infinite number of possible facts by a writer whose prime interest was her hero's plight. Does the "peeling" have any connection with him?

Troubled: Well, he doesn't take very good care of himself. He's in the stream of time too, and sort of a derelict. Isn't there a limit to this kind of analysis?

Me: There is no limit to what the imagination does, only a limit to our own abilities to follow it. I wonder if all that hot sun on his neck (line 19) might make his skin peel.

Troubled: You told me not to be cute!

Me: I didn't mean to be. Guess I got carried away and committed the famous critical error called being "farfetched." That's straining to find something that is not there. If my "insight" does not convince you and other readers of its rightness, I must be wrong. The watch the hero has abandoned (lines 3-4) is more obviously relevant to the theme of time. I prefer looking for connections that don't quite hit me in the face. Is his pitching the coffee grounds back into the river (line 28) a suggestion of hope for him? Is the swampland he plunges into (line 30) something between the water and the world of solid earth his father inhabits? Au Sable (line 11) is a place, is it?

Troubled: Yes, I've heard of the name, in Wisconsin I think.

Me: Could it be, or have been, "Eau Sable"? French for sandy water?

Troubled: I don't know any French. I thought it meant black in English.

Me: Yes, it does. Black like the river, and the coffee, like the "dark pools" (line 15) where the trout live. There is blackness all around in the poem, and there is a triumphant escape from it.

That is what the younger man has to look foreward to, his own emancipation from the past. Yet the landed trout, the one forcefully taken from the water, dies. The son cannot be pulled out. He must break out on his own, in his own good time. For now, he seeks the trout's "dark pool," not an escape from it. This stalled equilibrium is at the center of the poem. In a sense, the climax of the poem is when the trout "lunges, / Bursting in urgent spatterings / of silver and brown" (lines 15-17). We must find how that connects to our hero.

Troubled: I'm sure it does connect but I can't say exactly how.

Me: Nor I, exactly. But since your poem has to do with the intimate and troubled relationship of father and son, we should expect some of its imagery, like this "Bursting," to reflect its oedipal tensions in sexual imagery. Is this too much for you?

Troubled: Not too much, but quite enough thank you.

Me: Thank you: It is a fine poem. I need to read it some more.

Troubled: Me too.

CHAPTER SEVEN

Authors and Heroes

Talking about it is easier than doing it. You have been so industrious that you deserve a little rest. Take it easy while I talk about it some.

In the last chapter, I tried to prompt a writer's imagination by having her put down on paper a mass of specific information about her as yet unwritten poem's central character and the place, or setting, of the poem's action. The questionnaires I have devised force a writer to look out into the world of his imagination and to focus his powers of attention on the specific data of a limited case or situation. This procedure is essential to all creative writing, although experienced writers have internalized the questionnaires. They fill them out in their heads without thinking about what they are doing, and they invent and refine specifics of their case during the process of writing, not all at once, and not all before they begin to write. For some inexperienced writers, the questionnaires will be helpful, and there are many fine poems that exactly correspond to their prescriptions. There are, however, many poems that do not seem to.

There are many poems that appear to have neither a hero nor a setting nor a specified time and place. Numerous fine poems, and some great ones, give us only an unidentified person describing an inanimate object in an unspecified place and time. And there are poems of the highest value that present a central character who is utterly despicable or downright boring—not at all our superior.

How to Write a Poem

One resolution of the apparent contradiction between my questionnaires and poems of those kinds is that the questionnaires are pedagogical devices or tools; like all teaching aids, they distort the nature of their subject. They are to be used, in those instances where drastic methods seem required, and discarded as soon as they have done their work, or been given a chance to do so. The beginner, once started, will break through the limits of any system, however useful it has been, however comforting and tempting it always is to have clear-cut instructions to rely on.

Despite these qualifications, however, it is true that every poem must have a hero in it, a character of central importance to the poem. The hero is not necessarily central in importance to the plot or story. He doesn't have to be heroic in the usual sense of that word, but he, or of course she, has to engage our interest throroughly. By our "interest" I mean something larger than curiosity, pity, or even sympathy. To be a poem's hero requires sensitivity—moral, perceptual, intellectual, and/or intelligence in at least as high a degree as the reader—and/or highly developed moral virtues. The hero is at least as admirable as we are, and he has the added advantage of knowing something we don't know, or of having experienced something we have not. The hero earns our respect, admiration, even awe.

A complicating factor in all this is that a poem's hero is quite likely to be not a person described in the poem but the person who does the describing. There is a good deal of potential confusion in that statement. There are *no* people in poems (or novels or plays). What seem to be people there, what we casually think of and refer to as people, are, in fact, characters. Characters are literary versions of people, and they are always drastically simplified versions. No matter how complex a character is, no matter how "true to life" we say a character is, a moment's reflection will show us that his admirable complexity and verisimilitude (that will be sixty-four dollars, thank you) fail to capture the complexity and vividness of any living and breathing person. Literary creation cannot compete with the other kind—so it does the next best thing: it aims to create an illusion that, at least for a little while, readers are willing to accept as the real thing. The only thing a literary creator can create is a work of literature.

Authors and Heroes

Characters are not people—nor, for that matter, are striking passages of description what they are often called, in praise. They are not pictures. Literature does not give us experiences of the same kind we get from the life of our senses.

Undoubtedly the most important point of confusion between life and art has to do with the character who acts as the narrator of a poem. (The narrator may also be called the speaker.) The narrator is a character, not a person, not the author. I know this sounds odd, if not plain wrong. John sits down at his desk intent on telling us about himself. He writes of himself as "I"—he may even write of himself as "John." But in the process of condensing himself so that he can exist merely in words—usually in a small number of words—John-the-author cannot avoid simplifying himself, leaving things out on purpose and/or as a result of his limited knowledge of himself. The version of John-the-author that comes to exist in a poem is not John-the-author but John-the-narrator. John-the-narrator is a character in a poem written by John-the-author.

The speaker, or narrator, of a poem may be its hero, or the hero may be some other character in the poem. Believe it or not, there are poems in which the speaker seems to be the only character, in which that speaker is not the hero—yet the poem does have a hero! How can this be? Simple! A poem goes like this: "I am John Doe, and here is what I did yesterday. Pay attention to what I tell you and you will see what a good fellow I am." So we read the poem and discover that John Doe is not a good fellow at all. We read what he says—he is the only person who says anything in the poem—and learn that he is the scum of the earth. Who is the hero of this poem? Surely not the despicable character who is the narrator. Who's left? Who is it that devised and executed this devious strategy? Who is it that created the narrator in such a way that readers soon discover that he is a bum? You are bursting to answer that question, I think. You want to say that the hero of the poem is the person who wrote it, that the hero is the author.

Your common-sense answer is satisfactory for most purposes, but it contradicts the principles that the poem's hero is a character "in" the poem and that a character is not a person.

While we are reading the poem in which John Doe tells us he is a good guy but accidentally *shows* us that he is a bum, we sense the presence of somebody else—somebody who is pulling the poem's strings, an invisible ventriloquist whose laughter at John Doe, though of course silent, we, in some sense, hear. That invisible chuckling ventriloquist is "in" the poem. Is he identical with the author of the poem, or is he a creation of the author? He is an invented creation of the author. Unlike the author, our ventriloquist exists only during the course of the poem. He is born with the poem's birth, and he vanishes at the end of our reading of the poem. A name for this ventriloquist, this character who is the poem's hero without saying a single word out of his own mouth, is "the implied author." He is an invented version *of* the author *by* the author. He is a character in the poem. His existence and his nature is implied by the poem's text—something like the way the existence and nature of the force of gravity is implied by that apple that falls from tree to head.

The author of a poem is, in a sense, always a hero because he wrote the poem, but the author is not a character, nor is he *in* the poem. The author's name may appear on the page, but that name is not a part of the poem. The poem's existence is not affected by our knowledge of the author's name. The only part of a poem that may be credited to the author directly, the only utterance that may come to us directly from the author is the poem's title. Like most theoretical matters, this discussion has only an indirect bearing on the poet's task. It can be helpful to us as readers of poems, and since we read and reread our poems during their composition, it can help us write them. It can help us talk about them. For example:

Blood Bank Refugee

It's Monday	1
and I am in this place	2
again.	3
Bad breath, bleary-eyed,	4
coughing and spitting, too.	5
I am out of wine;	6
It happened Friday, late;	7

```
    cigarettes too.                             8
I am at the blood bank.                         9

That girl behind the desk,                     10
    Ain't she somethin'                        11
    Ain't she?                                 12
Twenty years ago                               13
I'd 've chased that girl,                      14
Caught her too,                                15
    you c'n bet!                               16

But now                                        17
She looks at me                                18
    and smells my breath                       19
    and stands way back                        20
```

The speaker in this poem is a wino, a derelict, who has gone to sell his blood to replenish his wine cellar after a weekend of enforced abstinence. As winos go, he is, I suppose, a superior sort. He speaks better than we might expect. He is high-spirited and not at all threatening. He has enough self-knowledge to feel some superficial remorse. He is not unpleasant company; the bad breath, coughing, and spitting he speaks of do not discomfort us as they might if the man himself, and not the invented character, were before us. But the bum is not an adequate hero. We may wish him well, but we do not admire him for his moral or intellectual excellence. He is not our superior. He boasts about his old virility and competence (lines 13-16) in the context of his present condition. He asks the reader to admire him for what he was and even for his ability to remember it. We are asked to pity him for the contrast between his past and present states. The girl behind the desk recoils from his countenance and his bad breath, and as he tells us that, he means: "Isn't it terrible what has become of me, terrible that this lovely girl dislikes me? How very sad a case am I." He begs for the reader's attention and pity. No booze, no cigarettes, no Listerine, no money, and to cap it, no admiration from the girl. "Feel sorry for me," he orders his readers, "*I* feel sorry for myself." No, a character who behaves like this cannot be the hero of a poem. (Perhaps we *can* admire him some for his philosophic outlook, his awareness of his plight, his self-knowledge, such as it is. I do not find very much of these qualities in him, and if you find much more of them our evaluations of the poem will differ. I think yours will be inferior and that we could profitably discuss the question. I think I would win, that is, would convince you that I am right.)

Let us assume that we agree that the derelict is not an adequate hero and ask ourselves, "Who is?" Surely not the girl behind the desk. The author is left, but I have just argued that the author cannot be a poem's hero because he is not *in* the poem. Just as the speaker who calls himself "I" is not identical with the author but is a character invented by the author, so is the person who, among other things, wrote the poem, not identical with the presence that we feel living behind the words of the poem. We feel the presence of that invented, implied author as we read the poem. Someone else is in our head as we read the poem, someone who doesn't say a word—except perhaps the poem's title—but who has created the people and actions of the poem and who hovers in and around it. It is that presence who is our last candidate for the job of hero. That's all he does. He has no life outside the poem. Does he have enough life *in* this poem to be an adequate hero?

You: I'm back.
Me: I'm glad.
You: And I think I understand all this, even the complicated rigmarole about the implied author, but what's the point, and how will this help me to write my own poems?
Me: I don't know that it will help you write your poems. I am explaining one of the ways poems work and one of the ways they are judged. Maybe having this in your head will help your imagination do its thing. Writers are also critics, whether they like it or not. You don't write your poem in one nonstop sweep. You stop, often I expect, and read over what you have already written. As strongly as I tell you not to think about your poem but to devote your entire energies to the imagined persons and places you are writing about, I expect you will disobey me. You will find yourself staring at the words on the page before you and wondering what to do next. Is it any good? Is it fixable? Is it finished? You have by

now eight rules to guide you at that point. Rule 9 may help too: a poem must have a hero. But only after you know what a hero is and where he can be found.

You: The hero of "Blood Bank Refugee" is its implied author, right? Not Joe Smith who wrote the poem, but the version of Joe Smith that Joe Smith invented to be his ...

Me: Mask. He, the implied author, is the only version of Joe Smith that is in the poem and therefore known to us.

You: What if the real Joe Smith is a friend of mine? Do I pretend I don't know him when I'm reading the poem?

Me: You couldn't do that, even if you tried. But to say you know the real Joe Smith personally is not a simple proposition. You surely do not know him perfectly. You are always liable to be surprised by him; you are never sure you know what's going on inside him. You *can* know the implied author perfectly. Everything there is to know about him is in the poem. The implied author is the version of Joe Smith you should pay attention to first and most of all. The question that matters is whether the implied author of "Blood Bank Refugee" is a satisfactory hero. Is he?

You: He sympathizes with the wino, and I can sense a kind of admiration for the old codger's ability to be enthusiastic about the girl behind the desk.

Me: He is called a "refugee" in the title, a person who has fled his home and sought refuge in a new place.

You: The word doesn't fit the case exactly, does it? We don't know anything about his fleeing his old life, and the blood bank isn't a new home, just a place to do business.

Me: Yes, the title is imprecise. Maybe a bit misleading and unfair. We think of refugees as victims of other people's persecution, and we do what we can to help them. By calling the wino a refugee, pity is sought for him that we have no reason to believe he deserves. The poem assumes that he, and all like him, are innocent victims, deserving unqualified sympathy. This assumption is a form of sentimentality, emotion in excess of the merits of the particular case. Something of the word "refugee" in the title rubs off on the wino, but we know nothing of his connection with political refugees, the most common refugees our times know. Does the implied author's sympathy and admiration for the wino make the implied author a satisfactory hero? I'd better answer that myself, since I have already started to do so by criticizing the title. The implied author is not a satisfactory hero. The poem does not have a satisfactory hero. It has many merits, but without a hero, no poem can be very good. The implied author of this poem is not, as far as I can tell, superior in any important way to the wino. He agrees with him, thinks and feels about things the same way the wino does. The wino says pity me and admire me; the implied author says the same things, and no more.

Another way to say this is to say that there is insufficient distance between the wino and the implied author. The implied author is not detached enough, not critical enough. He has let himself get carried away. Sympathy for our fellow men is essential, and I am not saying that one can be too sympathetic to people such as this wino. But sympathy that blots out our intelligence is an indulgence we should not permit ourselves. It does not do the object of that sympathy as much good as sympathy tempered with judgment and enriched with intelligence. What this wino asks for is sympathetic admiration. What we know he needs—what we suspect he really wants—is something larger than that. He presents himself as an object of pathos. He pleads for our pity. The implied author takes the easy and irresponsible way out. He fails to keep his distance, his aesthetic and moral distance.

Since the actual author of this poem is a personal friend of mine, it is very handy to be able to talk about the deficiencies of its implied author, and keep my friend friendly.

You: He is at fault, though, your friend the author, if the poem lacks an adequate hero.

Me: Yes, of course. But I can say that indirectly by talking about the implied author. The author fails as a writer; the implied author fails as a person. My friend can draw his own conclusions from that, and those conclusions will not be encouraging. The implied author has created a self-pitying, sentimental slob, and then cheered him on. There is no more wisdom or intelligence or sensitivity brought into the poem by the implied author than there was brought into it by the wino. What this poem badly needs is an implied author who sees and feels what the wino ignores, whose attitude toward life is larger and wiser, whose feelings are broader and deeper. I know that the actual author of this poem is capable of all those good things. He does not think self-pity is a virture to celebrate. He does not think the blasted lives of skid row bums merit only superficial consideration. But that's exactly what the implied author of this poem thinks. You are perfectly free to put a twit, a drastically inferior moral being, at the center of your poem's action, but you may not present yourself, in the role of the implied author, as another twit. There are all sorts of people who cannot be heroes of poems and who the implied author cannot simply endorse. And these sorts of people are the very sort beginning writers tend to write about. Beginners seem to instinctively find this way to evade their responsibilities and the pains it would take to bear them. They trivialize their characters, their poems, and themselves. The antidote to this cowardly superficiality may be found in our last and most important rule. I present it without explanation or apology. (Without arrogance too, I hope.) I leave it to you to interpret the rule as well as I know you can. Rule 10: Grow up. Or: Be your "Best Self."

The characters you may not merely present and endorse include children, fools, twits, the retarded, the insane, men from Mars, gods, devils, animals (even those that talk), moral degenerates, and the senile. And any sort of person, even one of heroic sensitivity and moral courage, cannot be a poem's hero if he is presented in a moment of violent physical of emotional action. When the adrenalin flows, the person's vital human will drowns. He loses self-knowledge and self-control. He becomes a creature of instinct. There are no heroes at such moments—in war, sport, frenzy. A hero can remember or foresee violence and think and feel about it. His thoughts and feelings, during an episode of violence, are inconsequential, blotted out by the pressures of the moment. He is, temporarily, what a child or a madman is persistently: thoughtless. If your subject is not a satisfactory hero, you must invent another character who is.

You: What's wrong with children?

Me: Only that they are childish. They are not adults. They do not have the virtures unique to morally superior adult humans.

They cannot be heroes of poems. Only a moral being can be that—either a moral being as subject of the poem, or as its narrator or its implied author.

You: You use the word "moral" a lot, in an odd way.

Me: An *old* way. "Moral: pertaining to conduct," but pertaining to conduct in the sphere of manners rather than in terms of ultimate good and evil. I'm not sure exactly what God expects of us and what He counts sin. I *am* confident of my judgments of how people ought to behave toward me and each other. I'll take the manners and leave other matters to higher authority. The poem's hero must know how to behave. (He must be an expert on Rules 2 and 3.) Neither the wino nor the implied author of "Blood Bank Refugee" behaves excellently well, and so that poem soon bores us. The actual author evidently failed to concentrate his fullest attention on his invented character. The poem insults its readers, and insults the wino too.

You: That seems awfully harsh. There is a touch of humor in the poem; it's gracefully done. I'm not sure I go along completely with your condemnation.

Me: Perhaps I overstate my opinion because I know the real author and what he is capable of doing. Perhaps I overstate my case in order to explain the theory dramatically. Will you agree with my condemnation say, 50 percent?

You: Done!

Fireflies

There were times:	1
On the back porch steps,	2
Tomato vines winding up wooden stakes,	3
Twilight lighting up the fireflies,	4
One star, unshy and shining.	5
Times,	6
When the words snagged within me,	7
Or tied what I had to say	8
In ribbons, pink and blue.	9

What I have to say is this: 10
Tomato vines were climbing in my back yard,   11
The wooden stakes and the fireflies shone,   12
One star had come out.   13

There is nothing else,   14
Nothing more to do but tell   15
How I got there in a used car,   16
Three days too late,   17
But tell what I said to him,   18
How I drank, made love   19
To a soldier in his back seat,   20
Nothing but wonder what it was I lost in Cleveland   21
That the fireflies still have,   22
Growing deeper as night comes on.   23

Me: Wow! Do you like that? Read it again, out loud, slow.

You: I do; I *think* I do. But I don't understand it very well. She doesn't tell us enough.

Me: No? the speaker remembers a scene from earlier days and remembers the difficulty she had then in saying how that moment moved her. Her words "snagged" or came out as prettified clichés (lines 8-9). At line 10, she tries again, and what words she does find are only the flat description of the scene—she has given up the attempt to say more. Even the charmingly "unshy" star (line 5) is dropped, too close to those pink and blue ribbons, I presume. And although her trip to Cleveland was an emotional crisis for her, all she does is sketch the exterior facts of what happened. She has given up on directly expressing or defining her ideas and feelings, and she can only wonder (line 21) about that still unformulated thing that she has lost and that the fireflies still have, the fireflies whose "shining" increases when everything that "night" suggests comes on. Is all that in the poem? Is it enough?

You: It *is* a moving poem, and . . .

Me: And beautiful. A good word, worth the risk of embarrassment.

You: Moving and beautiful. But shouldn't I know more about what happened in Cleveland?

Me: Her relationship with the man went sour. In frantic despair, she misbehaved. Surely you don't want to know that soldier's name?

You: No, I guess the point is that he doesn't have one, was anonymous. But she got to Cleveland "Three days too late" (line 17). For what? To prevent her boy friend's marriage to somebody else?

Me: Is that a guess?

You: Yes; a hunch, a guess.

Me: Never guess! *Never guess!* Trust the poet until you are sure your trust has been betrayed. Trust him to tell you all you need to know. We know that she arrived too late. How easy it would have been for the writer to have given us more details. She didn't. The fact that she didn't provide certain details helps us see that they are unimportant. Have faith that the details not given are not important to the poem.

You: Yes, the poem is not about what happened in Cleveland. It is about how the speaker felt about what happened.

Me: Right. She speaks, after the violent emotional events, back home from Cleveland, back home among the tomato plants. What the poem is about is her inability to find words for her feelings.

You: She says the right words snag or come out wrong, but they do get said. The poem *does* express her feelings.

Me: Would it be too much to say that the poem expresses the inexpressible?

You: A little too much.

Me: Yes, my phrase is rather "pink and blue," the colors of babyhood. All that happens is that the poem says indirectly, through poetic means, what the speaker knows can't be said directly. Does the poem have a satisfactory hero?

You: Yes, the speaker.

Me: Yes. The hero is the speaker, not the actual person who wrote the poem. (The speaker in this poem is also the poem's implied author, in case you wondered. When that happens, we have a lyric poem. The other kind, like "Blood Bank Refugee," in which speaker and implied author are not identical, is a dramatic

[98]

poem.) Can you say what makes the hero of this one satisfactory? That can be hard to do.

You: She's so cool under pressure. And she will say nothing at all if she can't tell the exact truth. I admire her ability to face herself, to try to assess things. She doesn't let her problems make her an unpleasant person, someone who makes us very uneasy to be with. I like the tone of her voice, and its pace. Can I call it "stately"?

Me: Why not? No self-pity here?

You: Oh, no!

Me: Are you sure you haven't fallen in love with her a little? That last line, its intimation of death—isn't that a little too much?

You: No, it's just right. She's earned the right to say that. It grows out of what she's been saying all along.

Me: That's persuasive, hard to argue with. But I'll try. Whatever her misfortune in Cleveland, it hardly seems serious enough to make this "cool" and honest girl think of herself as dying. Isn't it excessive, sentimental? Read the last stanza again.

You: It's still just right. The fireflies shine under misfortune, as she thinks she does not. Under pressure, in Cleveland, she did the opposite of shine. "Night" suggests trouble, not death.

Me: One more time, that last line: "Growing deeper as night comes on." Do you hear the way those last words are written to require a very slow reading, with a little pause before "comes"? It's like a funeral march. If I changed "night" to "twilight" the line would sound lighter, quicker, and have less dark implications. It would return us to the poem's opening (line 4) and to the problem of exression, not the problem of my-boy-friend-just-left-me-and-I-think-I'm-going-to-die.

You: That would destroy the poem.

Me: One little word?

You: Yes.

Me: You are an admirable young man. Wrong, I think, but I am not as sure of the point as you are. I like the speaker so much—though not as much as you do. I find her so considerate and well-mannered in what she allows us to overhear of her talking to herself (her internal monologue or soliloquy), that I don't want her to lose her cool, to embarrass us all, at the very end.

[99]

You: She doesn't.

Me: Well, that's what makes horseracing. You may be interested to know—maybe disappointed too—that the author of this poem, a woman of my acquaintance, is a troubled and clinically neurotic person. She is given to destructive and self-destructive behavior. She is, or was, given to fits of hysterical rage and to extended periods of sullen withdrawal. She is happily married—as happily as a person like her can be—and has two pleasant children. She is rarely able to be pleasant company herself. Her friends—and she does not have many of them—would not see any similarity between her and the speaker of this poem. What has evidently happened here is not as rare as you might think. The writer imagines, creates, retrieves, a special version of herself, what she wants to be, what she *is* at her best. In the process of writing the poem, she grows up, transforms herself. This extraordinary metamorphosis (another sixty-four dollars!) makes the poem possible. Some people think it also helps the author make herself, permanently, a better person. Poetry as therapy! It is an old and attractive idea, quite unprovable. You are free to believe in it. "Fireflies" gives you a lot to think about, doesn't it?

You: Yes. But let's change the subject please.

Me: Fine. Would you care to locate the hero of this next poem?

"ADC don't cover this"

Tuesday the retarded kid's yellow school bus driver	1
Hit the dog and didn't bother to stop.	2
Wednesday Mother put a homemade cast on one of the	3
Three mangled legs, and the dog whined.	4
Thursday she placed the dog in the bathtub	5
Where it sat in filth, pitifully stranded.	6
Friday night he found the dog	7
Wrapped in towels on the porch,	8
Pleading with brown dying eyes,	9
And he cried.	10
Saturday the humane society told him they don't	11
Gas dogs on weekends,	12

But they took the dog anyhow.	13
Sunday the dog sat alone and waited until	14
Monday when business began and	15
The gas was turned on.	16

You: That's awful, terrible. Talk about sentimental excess! Talk about bad manners!

Me: Oh. I thought it would make an interesting problem in identification of the hero.

You: Who cares? This poem needs burning, not analysis.

Me: Yes, it is, no doubt, a terrible poem, the . . .

Irate Author of the Poem under Consideration: I heard that! How dare you! Poor people are being destroyed by poverty and indifference, and when I try to do something about it all you "poets" care about is being "cool" and "beautiful" and making love in Cleveland. If you'd put your talents to improving things instead of ignoring the real issues, maybe the poor would be less miserable!

You: Maybe.

Me: Maybe not. All kinds of writers have been writing for a long time, and things don't seem to have changed much because of their efforts. Do you think it would help if we left the poem as it is, and published it, or put it on television?

Irate: It might.

Me: Anything's possible.

Irate: Well, do it! The poetry you say you like I *know* won't do any good. My poem at least tries. It could make people *care!*

Me: That's exactly what's wrong with it. It fails to do the one thing it was designed to do and what you claim as its justification. It won't make people care for anything except escaping from the poem itself. You can't bludgeon people into doing what you think they should do—and you shouldn't bludgeon them. (But I am very tempted to try to bludgeon some sense into *you.* How you add to the miseries of this world with your ignorance, thoughtlessness, impatience, your child's heart—and brain—your shallow, boastful cowardice!)

How to Write a Poem

Irate: Why shouldn't I bludgeon them? It's the only way to get some people to listen. Strong medicine is what they need.

Me: ("some people," "what they need." It's the fascist's theme song!) The medicine is too strong. It kills the patient before it gets a chance to cure the disease.

Irate: It can't be too strong!

Me: Okay, okay. Try it this way. What's wrong with your poem is that it isn't strong enough. With your permission I'll show you how to make it stronger.

Irate: You want to change my poem?

Me: Yes.

Irate: No! I forbid it.

Me: You'll still have your original version; it won't go away.

Irate: No. It's mine. Don't touch my poem!

Me: Bind and gag that woman and put her up against the wall in the corner!

You: Yes, sir! With pleasure.

"ADC don't cover this"
(revised)

Tuesday the bus driver hit the boy's dog	1
And didn't bother to stop.	2
Wednesday Mother put a cast on a mangled leg.	3
Thursday she put the dog in the bathtub,	4
Where it sat safe but stranded.	5
Friday night he found the dog	6
On the porch, wrapped in towels.	7
Saturday the Humane Society told her	8
They don't gas dogs on weekends,	9
But they took the dog anyhow.	10

Irate: You left out "retarded." The boy was retarded, and it was a school bus, not just any bus.

Me: Are you writing a police report or a poem? Do you want to change the way people think or merely tell them what happened last Tuesday?

Irate: You left out two of the three broken legs.

[102]

Me: It's stronger my way. Which is sadder, one dead dog or a hundred dead dogs?

Irate: What a horrible question!

Me: I'll give you the answer. One individual case is what people can respond to. The single instance is what matters in poetry and in the experience of us all. Statistics are inhumane and cold, beyond our comprehension. A gallon of blood only disgusts us; a drop may break our hearts. And your poem shows that you know this as well as I do: you wrote about *one* dog.

Irate: You left out two broken legs, and the gas, turning on the gas on Monday.

Me: The "gas" (your beloved "gas") is still there, in line 9. You didn't have to say it twice. No one would forget.

Irate: You can't be too sure . . .

Me: With some people.

Irate: Well, you can't.

Me: Do you have as little respect for the poor people you deal with as you have for the readers of your poem? Watch out! Grab that umbrella!

You: Got it! Take it easy, ma'am. Get the door, sir.

Irate: α#$%¢&*+ . . .

Door: Slam!

Us: Whew!

Me: Her poem wasn't utterly hopeless, you know. Once I calmed it down we can see that it expresses a bit of respect for the poor. It gives the mother more than pity, gives her something more important—dignity. Who's the hero of the revised version? I think that's a trick question.

You: It seems simple enough. The narrator, that sympathetic, understanding, and tactful observer, is the hero of the poem.

Me: Well, then to whom do you assign the title? Why the quotation marks?

You: The author heard the phrase somewhere in her travels among the poor and used it for the title. It sounds like a welfare official said it.

Me: I hope the welfare official would say, "ADC *doesn't* cover this." I want the phrase to be the mother's.

[103]

How to Write a Poem

You: It could be the Humane Society people, or would they say "doesn't" too?

Me: I'd like to see the mother as the poem's hero. She brings up the boy, without a father's help. She tries to care for the dog herself, and at last succeeds in talking the Humane Society into bending their rules about weekends. The author takes the mother's reply to her son's question and makes it the title of the poem. The poem is an expression of homage to the mother.

You: All that strikes me as a pipe dream. I'd believe it if I could, but I can't. The poem's author, that horridly insensitive bully, couldn't possibly have written the poem as you are interpreting it—or rather, as you are rewriting it.

Me: It is a brave man, or a fool, who sets a limit on the range of human possibility. The author's extreme reaction to criticism suggests that there is more to her than meets the eye. Her instinct might have been to admire and praise the mother. But suppose the author lived in a world in which the only acceptable attitude to the poor was a superficial and sentimental pity. Suppose our author had been educated, if that is the word for it, to believe that the poor do not merit praise, to believe that to admire such a woman would be an act of treason to her own traditions. But in the role of poet, something of her better nature survives this narrow ignorance. Disguise it as she will, writing the poem allows her to demonstrate a sensitivity she is ashamed of. No wonder she didn't want me to revise it.

You: Another metamorphosis (sixty-four dollars for me!) through poetry. A marvelous transformation into a grown-up! You think writing the poem brought out Irate's best self. A fascinating theory, for which you have no evidence.

Me: Look at the poem's last lines, especially the word "anyhow." Isn't that how the mother would say it? We hear her voice there, and in the title. The mother had explained to her son that the Humane Society costs more money than they have. Both the mother and the child know that the dog will die, that all that can be done is relieve its pain. They don't say this out loud to each other, but they know that the "this" in the title means putting the dog to sleep. The boy argues that the money can come from ADC—he thinks that is the source of all money! The mother knows "this" is not covered, but she either finds the money for the Humane Society or talks them into doing it free. It any event, she talks them into taking the dog on Saturday. Having failed to relieve the dog's pain by her own efforts, she finds relief for it, and for her son, by these other means. She is, in this ignoble situation and through these almost ludicrous events, a truly heroic woman. The narrator of the poem sees all this and is so moved by it that she offers the mother her heart, or more precisely, her voice. In fervid respect, the narrator merges with the mother, at the end, and speaks with her voice. The narrator and the mother are, at that instant, inseparable.

You: Wow! Do you really think our friend Irate had that in her?

Me: Stranger things happen every day.

You: But do you really think what you said is *in* this poem? Read it again, slowly.

Me: My, my, look who's taken over this show! But you're probably right. I'm mostly describing a poem I *wish* Irate had written.

You: But she didn't.

Me: Not quite.

CHAPTER EIGHT

On the Rocks

The invention of a hero, a character whose presence in the poem holds and rewards the reader's attention, is one of the ways poems get written. The writer who can give himself to the character he invents transcends his own self, reveals something of his own essence, and displays, to our amazement, the processes and fruits of love.

You: That sounds "religious."

Me: I know. I hear books slamming shut at this page already. So be it. I said this is "one" of the ways poems get written.

You: There are other ways to do it then?

Me: I don't think so, but there are other ways to talk about it, and it doesn't matter at all how you talk about it, or think about it, as long as you do it. The rules I've given you are as much rules of social behavior, of manners, as they are rules for poetry, but the rules could be phrased, as they usually are, in purely technical language. I think that the writer whose attention to his subject is lovingly passionate writes best when he utterly ignores questions of technique—ignores everything but this subject. But the process of writing also works the other way around. A writer who begins without a hero, or without much emotional attachment to his hero, can discover and express the grounds of such attachment through the rituals of technique.

On the Rocks

You: By writing well you come to *love* your subject, or hero?

Me: I am trying to avoid saying it again in that "religious" way, but yes. Whatever you say, if you say it well, is a poem. The language will not allow a poorly written piece to be a morally, an emotionally, or an intellectually good one. And vice versa. The language will teach you about your subject, about yourself, and about qualities with names you may be uneasy with. When a poem fails, its failure can always be shown to have been a failure of technique.

At the Summit

I pulled my bruised body	1
Over the last rock	2
And stood on top,	3
Muscles burning,	4
Aching, twitching spasmodically,	5
Lungs bursting,	6
Panting like a dog on a hot day.	7
Below: pines clung to mountainsides,	8
A green blanket to cover naked rocks,	9
To soothe and mellow them—	10
Rocks, otherwise, seething hot and harsh.	11
Below: sunlight danced on the river	12
And sent flashing mirror messages from the valley floor.	13
A curling snake, it twisted	14
Sliding long and lazy,	15
Green and cool,	16
Disappearing in the distant mists.	17
(I came searching for my soul.	18
Someone said I'd find it here.	19
Soul! Jesus, what is that?)	20
I lay back,	21
Letting the sun bake my skin,	22

[107]

Every muscle limp, sinking, melting   23
Into the earth to fit its contour.   24

I ran my fingers raw over a rough stone,   25
Like a blind man discovering a stranger's face,   26
Then comforted them,   27
Finding a soft, smooth patch of moss.   28

Wind batted my hair,   29
Bouncing locks   30
On my checks, then nose.   31
Air, so cool and gentle,   32
Swept my face   33
In a soft caress.   34

This is not a successful poem. It does not make the hair at the back of my neck stand up. It isn't even interesting. The implied author, the "I," is trying to understand what his mountain climbing means. A fine subject. I am glad "I" did not settle for the easiest way out: he could have announced at the end that he had found his "soul." But he is too smart for that. He knows that his soul, whatever that is, is not to be trifled with. He tries to define the experience by paying attention to the physical world around him and to his own physical sensations. (Of course our physical sensations are never purely physical.) If he is to learn something about that soul and about the meaning of his mountain climbing, he will find it in and through his own sensations. Your body may be, as they say, what you eat; your soul is what you see—with all your senses. The quality of seeing in this poem is poor, or, to put it another way, the quality of the writing is poor, imprecise, careless, inaccurate. The writer says things that are not true and that he knows are not true. We can hear his lack of confidence in what he is saying in the poem's music. It lurches, hesitates, stumbles. We could improve the poem's overall quality by improving its music, or improve its music by improving the quality of its seeing. That, I am sorry to say, could stand a good deal of improvement.

Enter, *Rocky, Author of "At the Summit"*: I was only doing what you told me to do, sir. And I tried very hard.

Me: I don't doubt that for a moment. But there is a kind of trying you seem to be a stranger to. Even if you tried harder than you ever did before, it was far from hard enough. I don't say it's your fault; you tried as hard as you could imagine anyone trying. But you didn't care enough about your subject to force yourself past poor writing, half truths, lies, and silliness. I'm sorry. Nothing personal.

Rocky: That's okay. Tell me more.

Me: One way to improve this is to improve your own knowledge of your hero by carefully filling out, or reconsidering, the "Hero" and "Place" questionnaires. Did you begin with them?

Rocky: Well, since the climber is me, I didn't think I had to.

Me: Aha! That will do it every time. Your hero, the "I" of the poem, is never simply yourself. The writer must know everything about his hero, often more than the hero knows about himself. And he must be sufficiently detached from him, objective, distanced from him, to see him clearly and intelligently. Nobody can be in this relationship with himself. For the moment, you might try what happens if you change the "I" of your poem to "He." You could get even further away, gain even better perspective perhaps, if you changed the "I" to "She." "She pulled her bruised body/Over the last rock." Read your poem through that way.

Rocky: That changes the poem a lot. Now I am in it as an observer.

Me: Yes, as a brooding presence. You report on what "she" thinks without necessarily feeling the same way. But even though "she" is the speaker, you "speak" directly too. For instance, who says that she let the sun "bake [her] skin" (line 22)? Whose word is "bake"?

Rocky: That's hard to say. I think it's my word, the implied author's word.

Me: And therefore his perception. Sometimes it is impossible to separate the voice of the "she" from that of the implied author. In those cases, we either have an insufficient distance between the two, or a case where the implied author has so thoroughly concentrated his attention on his subject that he becomes identical with that subject.

Rocky: Sounds like magic.

Me: It does. If and when it happens it is not because anyone planned it. Now I want to show you another way to improve your poem. Change the "I" to "He." Do not attempt to know him or meditate on him. That will be a by-product of your going through the poem very carefully and eliminating every word that is unnecessary and changing every word or phrase that is inaccurate or misleading or incomplete. Let's go. What gets changed first?

Rocky: The word "spasmodically," line 5.

Me: Because you have already said "twitching."

Rocky: Yes, I can take it out if you want, but I don't see how it hurts any.

Me: I do. Leaving it in says as clearly as can be that the narrator doesn't care enough about his hero. If he cared, he would not have time or breath to waste on the unnecessary. There is an economy that comes from, and proves, the urgency of caring. Good-bye to "spasmodically" and good riddance. What else?

Rocky: "soft caress," line 34. That *is* silly. Soft is the only kind of caress there is.

Me: Good. It is the kind of silliness that comes when you push. You want your poem to have more emotion, or a different emotion, than it has. So you pump it up with words like "soft," words that you try to sneak in for unearned emphasis. Any good reader will see what you're doing, and his response will not be "soft." A poem discovers and earns its emotional power. If you try to sneak in an unearned emotion, to pump up your balloon with air, you are sure to fail.

Rocky: Is the poem better now?

Me: We have barely scratched the surface! I'll go through the poem and show you some of the things that need fixing. But you will have to do the fixing, and it is less easy than merely removing an unnecessary word. In every case, what we remove or change affects the way the lines sound, and affects many other parts of the poem. A poem is a web of connections. Every part of it, in theory at least, is connected to every other part. It is like a complex machine, an elaborate carburetor. Any change requires retuning the entire mechanism. But that makes it sound harder than it is. Let me show you some places that need attention: "bruised body" (line 1). Is the entire body bruised, every square inch of skin?

Rocky: No, his body has some bruises on it.

On the Rocks

Me: Good, not the entire body, but bruises on arms, their undersides. From scraping against rocks or against ropes? If the bruises matter, tell us about them more accurately. "Over the last rock." I bet the word "rock" is not the right word. He pulls some part of his body over it, not his entire body over it, and "rock" is quite vague. It must be a very large rock, one he had to go over, not around. Is it really a rock, or is it a ledge? Or a lip sticking out over air at the mountaintop? Be much more specific. "Muscles burning" (line 4): All his muscles, or was he aware of only a few of them? Which ones felt that way? Did the burning sensation begin when he stood up on the top, or had it been there all along but only noticed when he stretched? Did all the muscles he was conscious of burn and ache and twitch, or did some muscles do one thing and others do something else? Did that twitching continue long, or did it come to his consciousness at the moment of reaching the top and then slowly taper off? I will not ask you if his lungs were in fact "bursting." You mean they felt as if they were in the act of bursting, or as if they were about to burst? What does that feel like? Have you ever had that feeling yourself? Can you tell us what it felt like? A person who had experienced this remarkable sensation in his lungs would surely do better than just the single word "bursting." That's the way someone who has *not* had the experience would describe it. Did that sensation in his lungs frighten him, or make him feel good, or make his head swim? Tell us. Your hero is not like all those people in second-rate books whose lungs "burst." He is unique, and your job is to show us that he is. "Lungs bursting" is a cliché, somebody else's language that has been used so often it is nearly worn out. Your man deserves his own words. Your readers deserve a report of his experience, not a phrase whose source is not the experience of climbing but the experience of reading about climbing.

Rocky: I stole that phrase?

Me: We say "borrowed." It's nicer than stole, and I doubt you borrowed it from a particular source. You had heard the phrase many times, without being aware that you had heard it many times. It has become a habit. But your mountain climber matters enough to be described in words that are not habitual. After you have attended to your man's lungs, you will have to see about that panting dog in line 7.

[111]

How to Write a Poem

When you tell me that the climber is panting, I am obliged and quite willing to believe you. I am a bit curious to know *why* he is panting. That hurried gasping for breath is common enough, especially after violent physical exertion, like a race at a track meet. Mountain climbing, as far as I know about that sport, does not require violent exertion. The climber goes very slowly, stops completely, often, to consider his next step, and to catch his breath. Why should this mountain climber be panting? Is it the altitude? He pants "like a dog on a hot day." Do I know more about exactly how he pants because of the comparison with the dog? No, I think not. Everybody knows how a human being pants. Everybody knows how a dog pants. Is your point that the man pants more like a dog than like a man? No. What is your point, then? I think the dog is padding, more air being pumped into your story. "Oh, the cute little dog; oh, the poor little pup—so hot and miserable, and so cute and pathetic." The dog brings all that into the poem and attaches it to your climber. Do you want those feelings for your climber? Or did you want nothing more than to make the fact of this panting clearer, more convincing, more important? The plain fact is given by the word "panting." You can trust your readers to notice it and believe it. If you wanted the panting to be more vivid, more exciting, even more pathetic, the dog is the lazy way to do it. If you were to ask a hundred people to make up a sentence with the verb "pant" in it, I bet ninety-seven would put a dog in it. It is the most common instance of panting there is. Poor writers take the lazy way. If something rocks, they say it rocks like a cradle, even if its rocking is not very much like a cradle. If something is black, they say it is black as pitch, even if it isn't exactly that color, even if they don't know what pitch is or looks like. And when a person pants, they say he pants like a dog on a hot day. Not only does your climber *not* pant exactly like a dog, his panting is not exactly like anyone else's, not even like his own panting on some other day. How do his cheeks move; what sounds does he make; where are his hands while he pants; does the panting begin slowly, get faster, then stop abruptly; or does he deliberately and obviously control its onset or its pace? How is his head held; what do his eyes focus on; is his nose red, his complexion pale?

[112]

On the Rocks

I see a stunned look on your face, and I can well understand it. I have fired questions at you nonstop. I have spent much more time and energy on your poor dog than you spent writing this whole stanza. I have, in a word, made a federal case of it. Part of the reason I have made so much of this line is that *you* didn't make *enough* of it. You described the climber's panting with no more exactness than is possible with the single, rather general word "panting." That did not satisfy you—you wanted to stress the fact. But instead of looking at your climber, instead of seeing and hearing him, you reached for the nearest phrase in your head that had to do with panting. You got a cliché—and this long dissertation of mine.

Another reason for that shocked, flabbergasted expression on your face is, I suspect, my own peculiar manner of discussing your poem. The questions come pouring out of me as if they were addressed to you, but I don't wait for your answers. I am, in fact, asking most of these questions of myself. I am trying to understand your poem and have been doing this out loud in order to show you what I mean by "understanding" your poem. I would have as many questions to ask myself if I were trying to understand a great poem. But the answers to *them* could be found in the poem itself. I ask myself questions about the poem in order to alert myself to the answers that I should find *in* the poem. Once the author has written the poem, his turn for answering is over. What I want to know must be found in the poem, not supplied, in conversation, by the author himself. The only way an author should respond to my questions is to show me where in the poem the answers that I have overlooked are to be found. After all this, I hope you see how the details of your first stanza need to be pretty completely overhauled.

Rocky: I sure do. I couldn't believe you were serious about that panting dog. But I see that you were, and that I wasn't. And you could have done the same job on other lines in my first stanza. Tell me more.

Me: Delighted to. Let me look at your second stanza as a unit. The climber, looking down, sees the pine trees. He says they cling to the mountainsides. (Shouldn't that be *one* mountainside? He couldn't see all the sides of the mountain at once, could he?) He says they are a blanket meant to cover the rocks, to comfort them. Is that roughly what's in that stanza? That question's meant for you.

Rocky: Oh. Yes, he sees that the rough path he took up the mountain does not seem so rough when he looks back down on it. It looks gentle, serene.

Me: Thank you. The pines, of course, do not literally cling to anything. "Cling" is not merely a description of how the pines look but a statement that the pines *deliberately* hold on. Only a person or an animal could do that. Plants don't think or have intentions or desires.

Rocky: I can't say the pines clung?

Me: You *can* say it, even though it is not a true description of the pines. It might be a true description, however, of the climber. He has just finished climbing this mountain. It had been a difficult, dangerous, and frightening experience for him. Clinging to the mountainside is what *he* has been doing a lot of. Clinging is very much on his mind. I know that because when he looks down at the pines he thinks of *them* as clinging. He describes his own feeling truly in the course of describing the pines falsely. This maneuver is so common that it has a technical name: The *pathetic fallacy*. The idea of clinging is in the climber, not the pines, and to the degree that your phrase gives us this information about the climber's state of mind, it is a legitimate use of the pathetic fallacy.

Rocky: Whew! At least I'm safe here.

Me: Not quite so fast. In order for the pathetic fallacy to work, we must not get the wrong idea about your climber. I presume that he is not insane, not so obsessed with fear of mountain climbing that he sees clinging in everything. There needs to be something in the way those pines actually look that inspire him to say "cling." If, for instance, we knew that the roots of the pines looked, even a little bit, like human hands grasping or holding on tightly, "cling" would work as description of the pines as well as description of the climber's state of mind. The pathetic fallacy only works to describe a normal human being when it works as description of *both* the thing described and the man doing the describing. What do we readers know about how the pines looked?

What was there about those pines that prompted the word "clung"? We don't know. (I don't even know if they are trees or shrubs or bushes.)

In line 9, the climber sees the pines as a blanket. This confuses an already confusing situation. Blankets cling because of static electricity, or because of their surface texture, not because blankets can be imagined to be holding on for dear life. What does the word "to" in line 9 and again in line 10 mean? Answer: "in order to," by design or intention. The blanket wants to cover the rocks, or someone (God?) wants the blanket to cover the rocks. (Why rocks? Pines grow in earth, not in rocks.) The covering of the rocks is expanded quite a lot. They are covered in order to "soothe" the rocks. Why do the rocks need to be soothed? Are you quite sure you know what the word "soothe" means? What does the dictionary say? Are the rocks in pain or discomfort, in need of medical treatment? The dictionary will tell you that the word "mellow" has many meanings and uses. None that I find lets me make sense out of your use of that word.

The rocks of line 11 would be hot if it were not for their blanket of pines. How hot would the rays of the sun have made them? "Seething hot," like lava! Boiling! Can rocks, hot or cold, be harsh? People can be harsh; some things people do can be called harsh; but can a rock be called harsh? The pathetic fallacy helps us see that the climber remembers how difficult his climb has been and thinks of the treatment he received from those rocks as harsh treatment. But what is there about those rocks themselves that brings the word "harsh" to his lips? He seems to be quite far away from them. We are told nothing about the sharpness of their edges, or of their hardness or roughness of texture that bruised his arms. They are harsh because he says they are, and as much as we want to believe him, and to believe *in* him, we are uneasy about taking it all on faith. If only we knew more about those rocks, those pines, then we could *see* them and understand *him*.

Not only can't the readers see those rocks, the climber can't see them either. Lines 10 and 11 deal exclusively with what he could not see because of the blanket and his distance from what was under it. He doesn't see under that blanket, nor does he see in his imagination what is under it.

Was his climb up the mountain made more painful by the heat
of the day that made those rocks painfully hot to the touch?
What went on during that climb that led him to feel the rocks
were treating him harshly, intending him harm? Well, I need a
breather. And you do too, I bet.

Rocky: I had no idea what I was letting myself in for.

Me: Now you do.

Rocky: I could kick myself for being so sloppy.

Me: It sounds to me that you've got my point about precise
writing. I'll go quickly over the rest of your poem, even though I
may have nothing to say that you wouldn't see for yourself.

"Sent flashing mirror messages." How about compressing that to
"flashed"? The "it" of line 14 must refer to the river of line 12, but
the reader has to hunt for that reference, and when he goes
hunting, he loses a little faith in the author and takes his attention
away from the poem's content. Snakes have such an illustrious
history as symbols, as in the Garden of Eden, that you should be
wary of them. Isn't it enough to describe the twisting river, as you
do, and omit the comparison with the snake? "The river curled
and twisted."

It is lazy to say "lazy" (line 15) when you mean, and the rules of
our language require, "lazily." Does "sliding long" mean anything
at all?

Look how many "-ing" endings you use here, and elsewhere. Are
they necessary? Is your point that the actions described were
continuous? I don't think so, and even if that were your intention,
continuous action is less specific than individual events. Instead of
"Disappearing" (line 17), try "Disappears" or "Disappeared" and
listen to how those sound. We see things one at a time, not in
clumps or collections. The "-ing" ending usually implies a collection. In line 22, "bake" is a kind of comic exaggeration, the sort of
thing a person might say, with a laugh, about the process of
getting a suntan. Your hero wants to find out the meaning of his
experience. not to make idle banter about what might be an
important part of it.

"Every muscle" (line 23) is really a lie. Even if the climber, or
the narrator, were a physician who specialized in muscles, he
couldn't know that *every one* of his muscles was relaxed. In fact, I

think it is common knowledge that muscles come in pairs; one tenses and the opposing one relaxes. "Every" is pushing, puffing up, trying to give the facts a greater emotional weight than they deserve.

In line 24 you use the word "to" as you had used it earlier: "to" means "so that it will." The muscles melt into the earth so that they will fit its contour. Perhaps this is merely the bad habit of the use of "to" as an easy, all-purpose connector.

Rocky: It is a habit, and a bad one. My "to" is a lazy kind of "and."

Me: The next-to-last stanza describes the climber in an almost maniacal state. He had been calm, relaxed, and now he runs his fingers over a stone with such fury that they become raw. It is like a sudden attack of panic, but then it is compared to a blind man's feeling a face, an act that is not one of panic. Having hurt his hands on the stone, the climber then seeks to comfort them. It is very strange.

Rocky: Part of this is just a simple mistake. Line 25 should be, "I ran my raw fingers over a rough stone."

Me: That helps a lot; "raw" from all that climbing. Did he run his fingers over the stone on purpose, or did his hand accidentally fall on the stone?

Rocky: Both. The hand fell gently on the stone, then felt it, as if to caress it and to examine its texture.

Me: That sounds most promising. The mountain summit on which the climber stretches himself out: What is the nature of the ground there? Full of big stones? Grassy? Sandy? You don't like to tell us about the sizes of things, the rock of line 2, now this stone in line 25. Those words, by the way, are an amateur's way of describing the affair. Wouldn't an experienced mountain climber use more technical words to describe different kinds of rocks and rock formations? I have been taking your climber as an amateur.

Rocky: Well, he is. But even a beginner can draw distinctions between pebbles and boulders. I will. And I know that the moss in line 28 is "soft."

Me: Is all moss soft? Perhaps I wonder about the smoothness of it because of the word "patch"—"a soft, smooth patch of moss"; "patch" sounds rather rough. By the way, do you see how the moss here is related to the green blanket of stanza 2? In both cases the rocks are opposed by green materials that mitigate their roughness. The meaning of that may come clearer when you revise your poem. Don't try to force the matter.

The wind that appears at the start of the last stanza has evidently just come up. Perhaps it is the breeze that rises as the sun starts to go down and the earth cools, or maybe the climber had not noticed the wind earlier. It may not be exactly fair to bring in the wind for your last stanza, something like a mystery novel in which the murderer enters only in the last chapter. I'd be happier if your conclusion grew out of what was already in the poem, not out of something brought in at the last minute. But if you do everything else right by way of these revisions, the last stanza's problems will probably cure themselves.

Rocky: You didn't say anything about lines 18-20, the lines in parentheses.

Me: They are an embarrassment. How I dislike that "Someone said." That vagueness. As if our hero were so naive and impressionable that he needed someone to tell him that there might be some knowledge, some fulfillment to be gained by climbing to the top. Take those three lines out.

Rocky: Then how will the reader know that the climber has those questions on his mind?

Me: That is a very useful question. The reader knows that spiritual and philosophical issues are always being considered. That's one of the things that makes a poem's hero a hero. He is always alert to the relevance of his experience to larger issues. He may never talk about them directly, that is, abstractly, but we can sense that he is a deeply serious and intelligent person. If we wanted information about mountains, we would consult a geologist or examine photographs. If it were a matter of measuring stress, we could take the hero's pulse. But we readers of literature, like the hero of the poem, always want to make larger sense of our experience. That goes without saying, goes better, or only, without saying. That's why we read the poem and why you write it. We *know* that your climber is "searching"' for the indefinable essence of things because of the painstaking precision of his descriptions. That in itself tells us that he is a serious person, that the poem is not trivial. The three lines in parentheses I want you to throw away mark your hero as a child. Only in these lines does he sound like he's a somewhat advanced twelve-year-old. Don't push. You have a serious poem in the making here. There is no need to stand up and announce that your purpose is serious. We will always assume that unless you show us otherwise. Now go rewrite your poem.

Rocky: I'm going to go climbing this weekend; that should help.

Me: No! You already know more than enough about climbing and mountains. What you need more knowledge of is precise writing. You don't need to climb another mountain. You need to rewrite this poem. I know climbing is much easier.

Rocky: Easier?

Me: Much easier. But taking time out, deferring your writing until later on the grounds that you need to climb some more, is a typical writer's excuse. Writers want to do anything else but write. (They will even read this book.) They will climb mountains if they can convince themselves that it is necessary for their writing. A good writer doesn't let himself fool himself very often. Write the poem—*then* go climbing if you want.

Rocky: Wouldn't it help to get another look at the mountain, to examine those trees, and the rocks, again?

Me: No, it would not help. You have a memory. You have an imagination. You have already had enough experience to keep you writing for the rest of your life even if you never again get up from your desk. The only experience you need is the painful, bruising experience of climbing a poem!

You: I thought I'd rewrite the poem sitting on top of the mountain.

Me: Terrific! I'll arrange for full press coverage. Maybe we can photograph you at your work from the Goodyear blimp. Be very careful about what you wear. You might want to practice jutting out your chin and looking very serious—like pictures of poets in *Time*. Of course if it rains, we'll have to put it off. Sergeant, will you please send in some men. I want this man put in a room and chained to his desk. Station a man at his door and another one outside his window. Do not release him for any reason at all until I give you the word. If he gives you a poem for me, bring it to me right away. Now, please take him away. I'm doing this for your own good.

Rocky: That's what they all say. May I have my poem back?

Me: No. Start fresh, from scratch. Think about your mountain climber, who he is, what he sees and feels. Whatever's worth saving from your first poem is in your head. Take him away!

At the Summit
(revised)

He gulped cold pine air,	1
Hands stretched and cradling a knob	2
at the peak's last lip,	3
Waited, exhaling, and pulled himself,	4
his twitching knees,	5
Onto the summit.	6
Below, pines clung to the erupting	7
Contours of the world,	8
A green blanket, soft, from here,	9
Roots and rocks, and the earth's tug,	10
Unseen.	11
He lay back, his neck open to the sun,	12
And let his shoulders fall,	13
Let himself melt and fill	14
His pocked and gullied bed.	15
He could have cried for his fingers,	16
Bruised and scraped, tingling with echoing ache,	17
Which played crab, like a blind man's	18
Over an unknown face,	19
And found to his comfort one a patch of moss,	20
The other a valley of silky sand.	21
Below, in his mind's eye,	22
Sunlight danced on the river's skin,	23

Flashed light-bursts to him	24
In glittering coils.	25

Before long, he noticed the wind	26
That blew across him,	27
Sweeping leaves and needles	28
Into the rift	29
Between torso and tundra.	30

Quivering in light's light,	31
A blonde lock rose above his forehead,	32
Swayed, knelt, fluttered, flowed, fell,	33
To a rhythm for which he knew no name.	34

Me: Let him out, Sergeant, and give him a cigar.

Rocky: Better, isn't it!

Me: Wonderfully better, marvelously better. It is about feelings of special intimacy between man and nature. Your climber, as the speaker sees him, finds a kind of home, a sense of being part of nature. He surrenders to it, as you surrendered to the facts you remembered and imagined, to the sensations you experienced. You and the speaker and the climber himself attend to that lock of hair on his head with such intensity! It makes a fitting climax after a lot of careful perception and accurate writing.

Rocky: I'm too tired to talk about it. This is an exhausting business.

Me: Exhaustion is the right word. What you had to say is on the page—*you* are emptied. I could talk about your poem, and praise it, at great length, but I will limit myself to pointing out how crucial is the idea of gravity, "earth's tug" (line 10). The climber had fought it, and then submits to it as his hair and "torso" submit to the natural forces of gravity and wind. That's why he "cradled" the knob of rock in line 2. He sensed a bond between it and himself.

Rocky: But that's not why I wrote it. The word "cradled" is just description of his hands preparing to get the best grip on the rock.

Me: And the bursts of light (line 24) in his mind's eye are just a physiological symptom of his exhaustion; the ground is a "bed" (line 15) because he rests on it; the mountain, like a person, has "a lip" (line 3); his hand is like an animal, a "crab" (line 18), because these things look that way! You are not the first writer to have written more than he knew. What you intended is beside the point. What you put on the page is the only point. The words I have reminded you of, and many more of your words, convey meaning as well as facts. They collectively express the speaker's feelings and ideas. The best description, the most careful and accurate rendition of the physical facts, is always more than that, always full of larger meanings. Out of the infinite number of physical facts that you could see and describe, out of the infinite number of ways in which you could describe them, you selected a very few. You selected the things and words you did because they also convey the feelings you had in you to express. Feelings: ideas and emotions in one. This happens automatically, without your wanting it to happen or even knowing that it is happening. After the poem is written you join the readers of it, and should not be surprised to learn something from the poem as a reader of it.

Rocky: It's not so much that I am surprised at what I have written. I sensed that my poem was about the climber's reaching some kind of communication with nature, but I didn't think that idea had gotten into the poem.

Me: It did. You concentrated so completely on the ways things look and feel that some part of you had, and re-created, a mystical experience. Or a magical experience, if you prefer. I don't wonder that you are exhausted. Compared with what you have done, what we usually call thinking is a paltry activity. Except for your last line, the poem does no "thinking" at all. Only at the end is there anything like an idea in the poem. There the speaker pulls himself away from the sensations and perceptions of the scene and comments on its mysterious unnameable quality. Yet there is a kind of name, a definition, for the experience, and that "name" is this entire poem. The poem defines it.

Rocky: I wonder what my fellow mountain climbers will think about the poem.

Me: If I were you I would be careful about showing it to them. Most of them are probably so busy climbing mountains that they have nothing left over to climb this kind of mountain. They must be the people who said you would find your soul at the mountain-top (line 19, original version). People who talk like that don't find much of anything. Be careful with them.

Rocky: I'll send them over to you.

Me: One at a time, please.

CHAPTER NINE

Son of Getting Better

The Corner

Flatbush and Avenue J.	1
Large flakes of snow	2
were sticking to your hat	3
and catching in your lashes.	4
Your briefcase was in your right hand and	5
your left hand clenched and unclenched.	6
You stared, and I thought	7
it was at me,	8
until I got closer.	9
You were staring past me	10
into the traffic:	11
splotches of color and chrome	12
streaked by.	13
You saw your face reflected in car windows.	14
You didn't move,	15
Your left hand stilled.	16
It was almost as if the cold had frozen you	17
to that spot,	18
and you were dead.	19
But you couldn't be!	20
You were here in Brooklyn,	21
standing on the corner.	22

You were breathing and holding your briefcase.	23
You couldn't be.	24
I walked past you;	25
You had already	26
taken up enough of my day.	27
I didn't care who you were	28
or what had brought you here.	29
I did turn around to check on you.	30
I saw that DON'T WALK sign blink, and	31
I opened my mouth to yell at you.	32
The papers from your briefcase	33
were flying in all directions.	34
You betrayed me.	35

The title turns out to be a pun, a word we can take in two or more ways. The man with the briefcase is at the intersection of two streets *and* at a crisis in his life. For reasons we do not know, he has been backed into a "corner." The speaker is in a similar situation. She has sensed a connection between herself and the stranger, felt an irrational fascination with him. She fights it: he "had already / taken up enough of my day" (lines 26-27). But she can't resist her fate any better than the man can. She turns back to check on him and sees that he has walked into the traffic. With that, she unclenches her own fist, and immediately admits to herself that she had, in some odd way, trusted him, loved him. It was this that he "betrayed."

Look how true to experience that ending is, true to the speed and force of both automobiles and feelings. The speaker has only enough time to begin to call out a warning, and then the car has hit him—and the truth has hit her—and us. Splendid!

You: Don't you want to fix it, improve it, somewhere?

Me: Do you? I want to talk about it, to find out how it works. I see that the ending hit us as a surprise, but that it was there all along. We hadn't seen, we hadn't let ourselves see, what was coming, but we know we should have. ("We" means the speaker as well as the readers). The man is in trouble from the start: the snow is attacking him; his left hand gives him away. The traffic is there;

"splotches" suggests its ugliness, and "streaked" gives us its power-ful velocity. Splotches are things broken up and strewn about, like the papers from his briefcase at the end, like the snowflakes. I think those can be improved: "Large flakes of snow" (line 2) is not very vivid, or interesting. Line 2 could be "Snowflakes," and there wouldn't be much lost. The texture, size, velocity, color, shape, and density of the flakes is not here. All we get is the flat, vague word: "large."

You: We learn something about the flakes from the next lines, from the way they stick to his hat and catch in his lashes.

Me: Yes, maybe line 2 can be simply "Snowflakes" and lines 3 and 4 can be enriched a little. I guess his hat is a businessman's hat, felt, a texture that flakes would stick to. With a ribbon or band, and a jaunty flipped-down brim. If we knew a bit more about the hat, we'd know a bit more about the flakes. I wonder if the speaker was close enough to the man to see his lashes well. That may be a weak point. Could those lashes be big enough to catch more than one "large" snowflake each? Could she *see* this?

You: What do you suggest?

Me: I already did, or the poem did. The splotches and the flying papers tell us to do something with the snowflakes.

The crash, the meeting of man and car, is already there in line 14: "You saw your face reflected in car windows." The image combines man and car, and speaker and man—she sees what he sees, a most intimate connection. While we're at it, line 5 needs retouching. Read it out loud.

You: "Your briefcase was in your right hand and." What's wrong with that?

Me: Read it again and listen.

You: " . . . hand and"! The rhyme feels like an accident.

Me: If it does, we are distracted from the poem, lose some faith in the speaker, lose some confidence in the author. We could try to move "and" down to line 6. Or what happens if we replace it with a comma? Aha! What happens if we replace "and" with punctuation in line 5 *and* in lines 4, 6, and 7? There is an explosion of "and's" here. Does it help or hurt?

Large flakes of snow	2
were sticking to your hat,	3

catching in your lashes. 4
Your briefcase was in your right hand, 5
your left clenched, unclenched. 6
You stared. I thought 7

How's that?
You: Better. Stronger, surer, more controlled.
Me: I think so, less flabby. But before we decide, we should wait for the changes to the snowflakes, and hat, and eyelashes, and we should then read the whole poem through, with these "and's" out, and hear how it sounds. Do you see any weak spots in the second stanza?
You: Yes—"stilled" (line 16). That's awkward; "stopped" would be better.
Me: It is awkward, but "stopped" doesn't mean exactly the same thing. The word "stilled" suggests a quieting down, rather than an abrupt and complete cessation. But we don't use "stilled" that way: He stilled? The storm stilled? No. The verb needs something after it, an object. That is the nature of this verb. You can always rewrite the language, add to the dictionary, but if it sounds awkward, if it draws attention from the poem's content, if it lessens the reader's respect for the speaker, or for the author, you lose. I have another problem in the second stanza. Is the "cold" of line 17 a metaphor for the painful difficulties of life? Yes, of course it is, but is it *also* a reasonable description of the weather that day in Brooklyn? Line 17 suggests that it is very cold, cold enough to allow the speaker to imagine the man frozen, his left hand frozen, and his feet, the soles of his shoes, frozen to the pavement. Nowhere else in the poem is this corroborated. It is as if the speaker mentioned the extreme cold and forgot about it entirely. In line 23 the man's breath does not produce visible vapor. The whole last stanza is without any remembrance of the unusual weather. And those "large" flakes of snow, again, work against the idea of extreme cold. We think of that kind of snow going with fairly mild winter temperatures. Sleet, hail, and ice go with severe cold.

This second stanza is a preview of the events, and of the shock, of the third stanza. The speaker imagines the man dead, but "you couldn't be" she insists twice (lines 20, 24). That line is echoed in the closing "You betrayed me." How important and powerful is this rhythmic and metrical repetition!

> But you couldn't be!
> You couldn't be.
> You betrayed me.

The disappointment, the unadmitted knowledge of his impending betrayal, is all there in line 24. The third stanza is a meditation on what had already been given and felt in stanza 2. Wow! The third stanza can be a completion of the first stanza, too, once those snowflakes take on a bit more menace. This poem develops out of *itself*, grows like a tree!

You: Are you done?

Me: Me? Done? Why does it happen in Brooklyn, at just those named streets? Naming the place lends credibility to the poem—not that it needs this particular help—but does the specified location matter? Would any intersection in any large city do as well? Do we associate Brooklyn with anything that enriches our understanding of the poem?

You: No, but that may be the point. It is an extraordinary event that takes place, surprisingly, at a very unextraordinary place.

Me: Maybe. Yes, you have a point. I wonder if the place meant anything special to the speaker or to the writer. Is there some significance to the place in the private consciousness of the writer? If there is, I want it shared. Brooklyn is such a famous place, famous in so many ways. Which way is important for this poem? We can't tell; we can't understand that aspect of the poem, no matter how carefully we read it. That is a defect in the poem unless we *should* be able to understand why Brooklyn is the scene and have failed to read the poem well enough. If the point is that Brooklyn is an ordinary place in which an extraordinary event occurs, Brooklyn won't do. We do not think of Brooklyn as an ordinary place. Why not a place famous for its dullness? There are plenty of cities like that, God knows.

I want to point out that the speaker describes a past event and addresses herself to, talks to, the deceased man with the briefcase . . .

You: How can you be sure he was killed?

[128]

Son of Getting Better

Me: Because the whole poem moves in that direction, as we've seen. And the speaker speaks of him, and to him, as if he had died. We can hear that in her voice. If he had survived, the poem would tell or suggest that—and it does not. Rather, she mourns him. Right from the start she speaks of him as "you," this stranger. The poem is an elegy. It mourns not so much the man's death as the missed opportunity. He could have noticed her, and her interest in him, and responded by not betraying her. More important, she could have cared more, admitted earlier and more freely, that she did care for him.

You: She could have done more, spoken to him, held him away from the traffic . . .

Me: And saved his life, and they both would have lived happily ever after?

You: Well, why not? At least she might have saved him.

Me: You are a little uneasy aren't you, with the idea that the speaker is berating herself for not saving the man's life. How often do we read about wonderful heroic acts, by ordinary citizens, and see them on television and in the movies. It is one of the great sentimental clichés of our times, all those medals for all those volunteer firemen, telephone operators, spectators who turn into Supermen. There are even some new laws that pay people for their heroic actions, Good Samaritan laws. Yet, as you know, this poem is not like that. How much simpler it would be if it were, if the poem were based on the usual assumptions. It would be a much less disturbing poem if it incorporated the familiar idea that an ordinary person can respond to a crisis by immediate and successful heroism. We all know better, know that the convention is trivial. That's why it is so popular; it denies the unpleasant truth, encourages us to believe what we would prefer to believe, even if we don't.

You: I've lost you. What exactly are you talking about?

Me: I take your question as a dare. You know what I am talking about, but you would rather pretend that you don't know. Your question is an attack. It implies that I have been talking nonsense. Maybe it is your revenge for my calling lifesaving trivial. But I don't blame you at all. It is very difficult to admit that you know how false are the conventional ideas that surround us. We swim in an ocean of lies, of warm, sweet "bull." How disturbing to admit to ourselves that we think almost everyone except ourselves is an uncomprehending fool. It's safer to join them than to be the one soldier in the parade who is out of step. Many of those others hear the right music too, but they are afraid of the marchers around them. So everybody marches out of step to the music they hear. A great and horrible comedy!

You: Will you please tell me, plainly, what you are talking about?

Me: Don't you have any idea?

You: I do have a hunch, but I'm not sure I'm thinking about what you are talking about.

Me: You are.

You: I'm not sure I am.

Me: You are, rest assured.

You: Why won't you tell me?

Me: Because you know it all yourself already. If you don't know, my telling you wouldn't do any good. You wouldn't believe a word of it.

You: Tell me anyway!

Me: Come in here and shut the door. Pull that chain across it. Ready?

You: Shoot.

Me: Nobody ever saves anybody's life; life can be extended, not saved. Everybody dies. And the extension of life, so many additional heartbeats, is not of itself the only or the most important value. The difficulties of life are not all medical. The physicians do what they can, then leave the harder, less mechanical, less trivial difficulties to us. Whatever led the man with the briefcase to his suicide is his fate, not symptoms of some curable or even identifiable disease. He is not a patient, a clinical example. He matters to us because he is normal, one of us. What oppresses him is called mortality, the human condition, man's fate. Only a fool or a madman would think about a cure for *that*. The speaker in our poem is interested in the man, attracted to this stranger, because she notices, or senses, in him, the mortality she shares with him. What is called for from him is not betraying her. What *she* could have done was to have less hesitantly acknowledged his importance to her. If you want to believe that a more generous response to the man would have communicated itself to him and that knowledge of her sympathy would have encouraged him to extend his life, I can't stop you. But that is, at best, an optimist's daydream. The poem says nothing about such possibilities. It assumes that the only possibilities that matter have to do with the acknowledgment of the human condition, not with attempting to escape it. Lead is heavy, no matter what we do or think about it. The only thing we can do about its weight is acknowledge it. The poem that started all this talk is an acknowledgment of human mortality and frailty. It offers nothing else.

You: It faces the truth that we are all incurable.

Me: Yes. It doesn't announce or proclaim that truth. It assumes it to be true and assumes that we assume it too. The assumption does not make this, or even help it to be, a good poem. It merely allows us to read it without immediate disgust.

You: You would not call the assumption pessimistic, I am sure. But many people would. Most people I know would call you a pessimist.

Me: Nowadays most people would use the newer jargon: "negative, a negative self-image." Most people, bless them, say one thing and believe another. They are very afraid of saying different things than "most people" say. It is not "negative," not pessimistic, to acknowledge the simple and obvious truth.

You: And it *is* the truth, isn't it.

Me: Don't get upset now. It isn't the truth.

You: But you have been calling it the "truth" all this time. How can you deny it?

Me: It is the "truth" of our age, the assumption made by thinking people, by the community of artists and intellectuals of our century. Other times have different truths. The "most people" you know are living on the faded debris of the assumptions of earlier times. The world sees different things, and sees them differently, in different eras. The "truth" is the shared assumptions of a civilization. We believe in it as long as we don't think about it that way. It is a convention, something like a cliché. It is the conventional version of the truth. To ignore it makes you either a fool or a genius born too soon. Poets, like anybody else, have to believe something. For us to read their poems, we must share their

[131]

assumed beliefs. Civilization, culture, wisdom are names for the consensus that allows this sharing. Nobody decides what a culture will believe. People who pay attention to their world make its culture. People who do not pay attention, and that is, I am sorry to say, "most people," sink. And as they sink they hurl rocks and insults at those who have managed to stay afloat. Do you understand any of this?

You: No. Mostly no.

Me: Good! It's like I told you. If you know, there is nothing to say. If you don't know, nothing *can* be said. But you did like the poem, "The Corner," didn't you?

You: Yes, very much. More and more.

Me: Then you "know." Its title, "The Corner," is really a reference to the universal plight I have been talking about. To state that we know that our beliefs are no more than assumptions is to threaten the usefulness of the conventions. A convention is useful only when we silently assume it is "the truth," when we use it without thinking about it. It takes considerable courage, a special kind of poise, to know that what you know you don't know but have merely assumed, to know that your house is built on sand. That's what makes poets' eyes twinkle. That is also why this poem, like many very serious works of art, allows itself the comedy of play, the playfulness of its punning title. And, speaking of poets, let me show you another fine poem.

Arthur

at the bulletin board	1
intent	2
(the same way he pretends to study at lunch)	3
sees me.	4
To be polite I say	5
"Hi Arthur how ya been?"	6
He wants more—	7
I see it pushing up under the skin on his face.	8
More would spring his:	9
Dodge Duster	10

New York Knicks	11
Air Force after graduation	12
And how he is really going to study now;	13
His:	14
financial troubles	15
knee operations	16
misanthropic boss	17
hassles with his old lady	18
and the girl who doesn't care.	19
His eyeballs jerk	20
back and forth across my face,	21
struggling to restrain my step.	22
If I let him	23
he'll clutch me,	24
suck on my sympathy for his	25
Dodge Duster	26
until he has it,	27
all of it,	28
and leaves me like the girl	29
who doesn't care.	30

You: I see why you showed me this one next. It was about what you were talking about before. It is about the incurable human condition.

Me: I'm glad you understood the poem so well, but I didn't set it up. All good poems, of our times, are based on those assumptions. This one, however, I agree, does make a point of the impossibility of helping poor Arthur. All the King's horses and all the King's men couldn't put Arthur together again. That puts a lot of people, and a lot of horses, out of work, so we hear a constant barrage nowadays from people who don't want to be out of work and who tell us about all the miracle therapies, all the guidance and counseling procedures, that will cure him. We hear from the horses too, I guess, or at least from their rear ends. There are a lot more horses' asses than there are horses! People can change, but we do not know how to change them. Goodwill is not enough.

How to Write a Poem

You: The speaker of this poem has the courage to say this.

Me: Yes, he does, but I don't think he thinks of himself as saying anything that most people would disagree with. His view is what people who write and read poetry believe—or rather, assume. He takes a very common subject—we all know people like Arthur— but takes his Arthur seriously, with a sympathy that precludes the comedy we might expect. (Especially if we have seen the movies in which Jerry Lewis plays characters like Arthur.) Do you see how carefully the speaker of the poem watches? He sees Arthur's "eyeballs jerk / back and forth across my face" (lines 20-21). He pays such close attention that the distance between himself and Arthur is momentarily abolished. Those lines imply that the "eyeballs" are not only seen but felt on "my" face. (I wonder if "eyeballs" is the best word here.) We have that same sort of miraculous closeness in line 8. The speaker sees a facial expression forming before it is complete; he sees the muscles churning beneath Arthur's skin. These moments in the poem tell us very convincingly about the intensity of the speaker's interest, about his desire to come close to Arthur. And they point up the weakness of lines 2-4. I guess Arthur habitually pretends to be reading when he is in fact surreptitiously looking around for—what would you call it?

You: Friendship?

Me: Sure, that's what we'd call it, maybe the best single word for it, but the speaker of the poem doesn't use that word, or any single substitute for it. Arthur's need would be diminished by putting a simple label on it. The speaker calls that need "it" (line 8), just as he calls his own sympathy for Arthur "it" (lines 27-28). It takes the entire poem to say what those "it's" are. We can talk about Arthur's need for friendship, but the fuller truth of what he needs cannot be expressed by anything less than the poem before us. That's why we needed the poem; no other set of words would say it as fully or as truthfully.

You: Line 3 refers to "the same way," but we do not know much about that "way." It is not described at all.

Me: Yes. Here the speaker asks us to write the poem for him, to draw on our own experience of our own Arthurs. But our own experiences are all different. The best we can do is to come close to what we guess are the speaker's intentions. This won't do. If the

Son of Getting Better

writer wants to tell us something, he has to do the entire job himself; he can't leave the work to us. Arthur's stance at the bulletin board is compared to his studying at lunch, but how he does that lunchtime studying we are not told. That could be, and should be, described, made vivid to us. The space that it would take to do that can come from deleting line 5. It is not necessary, and it is obviously a rather lazy simplification of the truth. It is something more complex than politeness that motivates the speaker's greeting. There is sympathy behind it, for instance, and the fact that Arthur's "way" of looking around has forced the speaker to respond.

You: The weakness of lines 2-4 caused the weakness of line 5. If the earlier lines were better, the weakness of line 5 would be even more obvious.

Me: Exactly. You are getting to be an alert reader. Any other weak spots in this poem?

You: Line 18 doesn't fit: "old lady" can be slang for wife or lover. Here it should mean "mother." I can't believe we are supposed to think Arthur has a girl friend. Girls don't care about poor Arthur.

Me: I bet the confusing or misleading "old lady" came from "hassles," another common bit of slang, a rather tough and knowing way of referring to one's troubles with other people. Saying "hassles" encourages continuing the phrase in the same slang style. Arthur doesn't use that kind of talk. That fact is a sign of his being "out of it," as they say.

You: But Arthur is not speaking those slangy words.

Me: Well, who is speaking them? Don't let the absence of quotation marks fool you.

You: The speaker of the poem is speaking them, but the list he compiles, lines 15-19, is made up of Arthur's words. The list really starts at line 10.

Me: Yes, the list is Arthur's list in Arthur's words, except for "hassles with his old lady," and one other word that sticks out and that also prevents us from assigning the words of the list to Arthur alone.

You: You mean "misanthropic" (line 17). Arthur wouldn't say that. It should be changed.

You: So that the list of Arthur's interests and troubles will

[135]

sound as if it were made up of his own words. The speaker is quoting Arthur.

Me: What about line 19? Would Arthur say, even to himself, "the girl who doesn't care"?

You: That's hard to say. Maybe the words should be changed to make them sound like what we're sure Arthur would say.

Me: You want the words of that list to sound like Arthur's words, even though they are said by the speaker of the poem. What would it mean if we readers could not tell whose words, whose voice, we are hearing? Would that confuse and disturb us, or strengthen our sense of the potential intimacy of the relationship between Arthur and the speaker? Arthur and the speaker become one, become inextricably commingled, indistinguishable, if we cannot tell their voices apart. The space between the two people disappears once again. Isn't that what the poem is about?

You: Yes, it is. That's why quotation marks around the list would be misleading. The point is that the speaker is both quoting Arthur and not quoting him, and that we can't tell these two apart.

Me: Or maybe we can see the two alternating in some places and can't tell in some other places. The speaker is both drawn to Arthur and repelled by him. If the author of the poem thinks of it this way, he will know what changes are needed.

There are other spots which require less elaborate explanation. Line 19 is grammatically unsound. Is Arthur concerned about "the girl who doesn't care," or about his hassles with her, or about both of these?

You: Probably the first of those. If he had hassles with her, that would mean she *did* care.

Me: I'd agree with you if I knew exactly what "hassles" meant, and I don't. Slangy phrases like that haven't been around long enough for their meanings to get settled. They are useful for indicating something about the world or the style of the person who uses them, but they rarely describe anything else with precision. Authors should not let readers misunderstand them.

You: Poor "hassles." It gets blamed for a lot.

Me: As it should. In a good poem, all the parts are closely connected with each other, and one weak part weakens many other parts. What do you think of line 22?

Son of Getting Better

You: "struggling to restrain my step." It does sound a bit forced, too formal, maybe. Why not "me" for "my step"?

Me: Wouldn't that remove the idea that the speaker's feet are poised and even beginning to walk away?

You: Yes, a little. But there is no other reference to the speaker's body in the poem except this little one.

Me: Maybe "my step" is being asked to do too much all by itself. If the feet matter, they should be brought to our attention more. Why not just "struggling to stop me"? The more I look at these lines, the more I see that the problem comes from "struggling." Is it Arthur who struggles or his eyeballs? How do eyeballs struggle? I knew I was uncomfortable with "eyeballs." "Struggling" is not description, but judgment, summing up, conclusion. There are so many ways to struggle. We know that there is a struggle here without being told again, but what kind of struggle is it? What does it look like? Find a better word than "struggling" and the other problems with the line will probably disappear.

Something is not quite right with the poem's ending. If the speaker lets Arthur bend his ear, he will suck all his sympathy and leave him *not* sympathetic. Arthur will pull the speaker to him, but that is not a reduction of sympathy but an increase of it. I think the word "suck" is used here in two different ways, and that, at first, masks the confusion. I understand what is being said, I think, but I suspect that I am able to understand because I am unconsciously rewriting this part of the poem in my head. The speaker's sympathy is diminished or exhausted because Arthur sucks on it, until he has "all of it." We can guess at the meaning of these words because we've read the rest of the poem. The lines by themselves are gibberish, an opportunity missed.

You For a good poem there certainly is a lot in it that needs fixing.

Me: There is, if our criticism was all good, and it probably wasn't. We might be suggesting improvements that are impossible or that would do more harm than good. Poems are, in the last analysis, magical. What makes them work is never simple. All we can do is grope around in them. Maybe something we say will be of use to the author, maybe not. Talking about poems is mostly good for *us*. It helps us read better and, in most cases, write better. The writer of the poem we are discussing usually is miles ahead of us. When he takes one of our suggestions, and the poem is improved, he probably had thought about the suggestion himself earlier. Or he would have found it, by himself, in time.

This whole process of writing and rewriting is such an interesting activity in itself—so similar to other more common and, I guess, more important activities—that few poets can resist writing poems about writing poems. They are always about something larger and wider than that, but their announced subject is writing poems. Listen:

The Poet at Two A.M.

Lying on the floor	1
in the middle of the room	2
a scattered half-circle	3
of used notebook paper	4
forms an umbrella	5
of	6
which	7
he	8
is	9
the	10
stick.	11
The back of one wrist supports	12
the bridge of his nose	13
The other arm bent over the	14
head	15
shields him against	16
the pieces	17
the fragments	18
and chippings	19
of rock.	20
Drool seeps into the rug.	21
The lightbulb burns from the ceiling.	22

Writing poetry keeps the poet from his sleep. His own work is like the heavy labor of breaking rocks. Bits and pieces of his poems fall around him. He drools, like a baby—he is reduced to that by the great pains he is taking. See how the very short lines (6-11) suggest the idea of words as small chunks of falling rock. And the way the words are set out on the page here, and in lines 17-20, reminds us of a halting, very slow, and difficult process. All through this poem, clues to its rhythm are not given by punctation but by the line divisions. When our eyes hit a blank space where the next word should be, we cannot help but pause.

You: The last line is disappointing. The light bulb overhead must be meant to remind us of the cartoon: a light bulb suddenly appears over the head of the deep thinker, and the discovery is made. Eureka!

Me: Yes, that last line disappointed me too. Even your casual revision of "overhead" for "from the ceiling" is an improvement. The inventor's light bulb isn't a very accurate description of the poet's desire to make his fragments of rock fly; "burns" feels right. What the poet wants is there all along, if only he could name it. The shape is in the rock if he can chip away its disguises.

Enter, Author of "The Poet at Two A.M." He crawls into the room. In his hand is a sheet of paper on which many words have been written and crossed out. He holds the paper toward us. We see his bloodshot eyes and some words that have not been crossed out:

Stars burn above. 22

Before our eyes he turns into Superman and spurts up and away through the ceiling that isn't there anymore.

CHAPTER TEN

Telling the Truth, a Review

What it all boils down to, the rules and regulations, the various ways of getting started, the painstaking reading and rewriting, is: tell the truth. Among the objections to that simple recipe are: Who decides what the truth is? Is there one truth for everybody, or are we entitled to our own versions of it? How can I know if what strikes me as the truth, is? How can I know the truth before I start writing?

These and other objections cannot be definitively answered, but they can be confidently ignored. Take "tell the truth" for whatever it means to you. It's commonplace meaning will do fine. Tell the truth as you see it and ignore the complications and the risks.

At the same time, do not let yourself forget that whatever truly happens, happens in a particular place and at a particular time. The weather, among other things, never goes away, and is always a part of the truth of what happens. An act of thinking cannot be separated from the person doing it; nor can that person truly exist, or be truly described, without reference to his history and to the time and place in which his moment of thinking occurs. Between you and what you see, between you and the truth, is an invisible and impermeable screen that distorts your vision. You can call the screen your ego, or the unconscious, or understand it by understanding how the psychologists say we perceive things, that is, through various mechanisms whose accuracy is never perfect and is always varying. What you see is always colored by what you are and what you want to see, and by the limits of your seeing and perceiving apparatus. The difficulty of seeing the truth about things is further complicated when you start to tell what truth you have seen. The words you use to describe what you see are always limited by your vocabulary and your literary skills. No matter how large your vocabulary or great your skills, the accuracy and truth of your report is limited and is distorted by the finite resources of the dictionary and by the grammatical restrictions of your language. Grammar, which makes it possible for us to talk to each other, seems to limit what we can say.

The more carefully we look at things, and more diligently we try to tell the truth about them, the closer we may come to telling the truth about them, and the closer we *will* come to telling the truth about ourselves. Poetry *is* a form of self-expression, as many people who know nothing about poetry like to say. However, the writer's self only gets expressed when he pays no attention at all to that self but devotes his energies to the impossible task of telling the whole truth about something or someone else. (The "self" that may get expressed is not fixed or single. It has many faces and is continually being discovered and created.)

To be a writer is to forget all about this, to believe that you can tell the whole truth about things and that your "self" has nothing to do with this process. A writer has no interest in his self. He is so fascinated by what he sees, outside himself and in his imagination, that he utterly disregards himself, his feelings, his opinions, ideas, judgments. But when we read the poem, we find that it works or does not work, that it is a good poem or a poor one, according to how well it conveys the author's (the implied author's, that is) feelings, according to how well it expresses his self. There is no way to short-circuit this process. The writer tries to do one thing, yet we judge him by how well he has done something else. The awkwardness of this situation cannot be avoided. It is not unique to literature. We do not find happiness (or love, or serenity) by striving for it. The painter, although he takes extraordinary care to tell us the truth about a bowl of fruit, tells us less about it than would a casual photograph or a visit to the supermarket, or one bite. His painting of the bowl of fruit is not primarily valuable for what it tells us about the bowl or the fruit or the light that falls upon them. The painter's painting paints the painter!

A poor poem, like a poor painting, is a failure of self-expression. It may be improved, but not by deliberate exposure of the creator's self. The artist signs his name at the bottom; otherwise, he "paints" himself by trying to paint the banana truthfully. A poor poem is one in which the truth of what happens is poorly told and therefore one in which the author's, or the speaker's, feelings are weakly, unsatisfactorily, presented.

Portrait

Stepping off the subway	1
Onto the half-lit platform	2
His foot kicks a crumpled paper bag.	3
Turning to the door, he sees a man.	4
The man is old looking	5
With his gray stubble and his	6
Dirty winter clothes.	7
He is sitting on a bench	8
His legs straight out, his butt	9
Half off the bench, back straight too.	10
The only thing curved was his neck.	11
It bent so his chin rested on his chest.	12
From his open mouth he was drooling.	13
The spit being sponged into his chest.	14
One hand, fallen on the wooden bench, twitched,	15
The other, hanging straight down,	16
Pointed lazily to the empty pint	17
On the concrete floor.	18

The title announces that the poem is a portrait. Actually it contains at least the seeds of several portraits: the man who gets off the train, the drunk on the bench, and the speaker of the poem. While the man who gets off the train observes the drunk, both men are observed by the poem's speaker. It is through the speaker's eyes that the author sees.

Telling the Truth, a Review

"Portrait" is not a successful poem, and there are, as usual, many ways of saying why it fails. Let us start with our speaker-observer but ignore for the moment the questions of the accuracy of his observations and the gracefulness and economy of his language. How well, let us ask, does the poem let us come to know the speaker? What is revealed to us about his feelings? What of his "self" does the poem "expresss"? Is he sympathetic to the drunk, and if so, what is the nature of that sympathy? Is he angry at society for driving the man to drink? Is he bitter about the man who got off the train, saw the drunk, and failed to come to his aid? Does he feel respect for the drunk, awe, anguish, pity, scorn? It is not up to the readers to chose between these possible responses, to prefer sympathy to anger or vice versa. The only attitude or emotional stance that we may find unacceptable in a poem is the absence of attitude. If the speaker, the central observer and potential hero of this poem, feels nothing, his readers are entitled to be disappointed with the poem.

This does not mean that the speaker's feelings should be either obvious or simple. His feelings may well be shifting and complex, a mixture of many emotional and intellectual elements. His feelings may be so strongly felt that the speaker may be deliberately trying to restrain himself, to control his sympathy, anger, or whatever. His feelings may be those of deep despair at the uselessness of protest. But if the speaker's feelings cannot be discovered at all, by good readers, the speaker is dead and the poem trivial.

It will not do for the speaker to baldly announce what his feelings are: "I was very angry at the man for ignoring the pitiful drunk," for instance. That is no more weighty than an opinion. It is the accuracy with which the scene and event are described and the imaginative leap with which they have been invented that alone could convincingly express his feelings.

It is important that we readers distinguish between our own feelings—about alcoholism or subways or concrete floors—and those expressed in the poem. Of course we will be affected to some degree by our own feelings about these things, but we can usually make allowances for that. If a reader of "Portrait" had once come across a relative or old friend on a subway platform and discovered that he had become a derelict, that reader might be unable to disengage his personal experience from the experience of reading the poem. That reader would be unable to read "Portrait" intelligently, much less to judge it. He should disqualify himself.

A poem is not a piece of writing designed to allow its readers to express *their* feelings, but an expression of its author's feelings. If you want to express your feelings, go write your own poem.

Because all readers have had different experiences and are sensitive in differing degrees to particular events and situations, they can help each other come to understand a poem they read together by sharing their responses to it. Other people's sensitivities help us correct and enrich our own readings of a poem. This does not mean that everybody's reading or interpretation of a poem is as good as anyone else's. Everyone is entitled to his own feelings, and those feelings may make him especially sensitive to a particular poem. But those feelings might also lead him to read the poem wrong. No one is entitled to confuse his own feelings with those in a poem. One of the tests of a good poem is that most good readers will agree about the nature of the feelings expressed by it. Where they may disagree is about fine points and nuances of interpretation. A poor poem, one in which there is little expression of feelings, gives its readers little to agree about.

(What does it mean when someone says, "I'm entitled to my opinion"? This can only mean, "I am entitled to *state* my opinion," but people often use the phrase to mean, "My opinion is as good as yours. It's a free country, isn't it? A democracy?" Surely not all opinions are equally good. Some opinions, like some poems, are better than others, some worse. But ignorance, widespread about the arts, may make people defensive, and then arrogant.)

Let me show you something of my efforts to understand "Portrait." I notice that the man who gets off the subway kicks "a crumpled paper bag" (line 3). Shall I take his kick to be accidental? There is no reason to think otherwise, and the platform's dim light (line 2) explains the accident. (But why is the light dim?) Was that paper bag the one that previously held the "empty pint" bottle of line 17? It seems reasonable to think so, or at least to try out that interpretation. Then, the man who kicked the bag had,

[144]

accidentally and symbolically, kicked either the drunk's possession, or his unwanted trash, or the immediate cause of his drunkenness. This may be a beginning of an interpretation. I will read on, looking for other things in the poem that will confirm or force me to alter this germ of an interpretation. At the end of the poem, the drunk "Pointed lazily" to his bottle. Was the pointing an accident, the mere result of the sleeping or drowsing posture, or was it a deliberate act of communication to the man who got off the train? What was it intended to communicate? Does the laziness of his pointing imply that the drunk is a lazy or a careless person, or is that laziness a result of too much alcohol? I notice that the "straight" posture of the drunk is mentioned in lines 9, 10, and 16. Surely this must mean something, must help me understand the lazy pointing. But what does it mean? How does it help? I am stumped. I turn to you. Have you seen something I have missed?

A glimmer of a hint of the poem's possible meaning, of its emotional context, has seemed within my grasp, but I can go no further. I need to have the answers to the questions I have raised about the kicked bag and the lazy pointing. If I knew the answers to those questions, or to some of the other questions of a similar nature that the poem raises in my mind, I could begin to discuss what I know about the feelings of the two men in the poem and, working backward, could explore what I ultimately must know: the feelings of the poem's speaker.

Where do we go to get the answers to these questions? We go to one place and one place only. We do not guess about the answers. We do not locate the author and ask him—he had his chance when he wrote the poem. We look *in the poem* for the answers to the questions the poem raises. If they are not there, they are nowhere; the poem cannot be understood. The answers are in the descriptions of the scene and the events or they are nowhere.

What is the author of this poem to do when I hand it back to him and say,"We cannot understand this poem. We can't tell how the speaker feels about what he describes"? The author cannot be prevented from taking our criticism as a personal insult and seeking readers of a more courteous disposition, readers who will tell him he has written a masterpiece. He will certainly find such readers if he seeks them.

Or the author of "Portrait" might take our criticism to heart and rewrite the poem so as to make sure that it expresses a coherent set of feelings. He may decide to make crystal clear that the poem is about the speaker's sadness at seeing the subway rider's lack of sympathy for his fellow man, the drunk. Suppose our author wanted to do that. He might begin like this:

> Striding off the subway
> The well-dressed man kicks
> A crumpled paper bag out of his path
> With a well-polished and expensive shoe.
>
> Turning to the door, he sees a man
> Of about his his own age, although
> The man's gray stubble and his poor ragged clothes
> Make him seem older.

Had enough? It is not going to get any better this way. The author has found an idea, the contrast between the executive and the drunk, and has decided that his speaker will express emotions related to that idea. This will explain why the speaker is saddened by the events he describes. But an idea is not an emotion. The author has thought about his poem and his thinking has turned up an idea: "Isn't it remarkable, and sad, that two men of roughly the same age, living in the same area, should be so very different—one an imposing success, the other the dreariest of failures. The gross inequality, the unfairness, is pitiful." Thinking brings us ideas; feelings come from experience; poems derive from experience.

What, then, can our author do to improve his poem? He can, he must, ignore everything we have said about the expression of feeling. We mislead him by talking about his poem the way we did. We would have served him better by doing what most critics do, either out of courtesy, trepidation, or wisdom. We should have talked to him about his technique. The poem succeeds or fails on its expressive force, but it also succeeds or fails on its technique.

Technique is what *writers* must concentrate on; *readers* concentrate on the poem's feelings.

"Portrait" gives us a very great deal to say about its faulty technique. For starters, we might say this: The change from present to past tense, with "was" in line 11, is confusing. It seems to be an elementary error in composition.

The writing is imprecise: "Stepping ... / Onto the ... platform / ... [he] kicks" (lines 1-3). Does that say what it means, exactly? Does he step and kick in one motion? Can a person do that? If what is meant is that his *foot* kicks the bag, this is what should have been said. (There are many other lapses into imprecise writing.)

Lines 5-6: "old looking / With" is very awkward. Does it mean old looking *because of*, or old looking *and*?

Line 4: What "door"? Trains have doors, but do platforms have doors?

Line 7: Is the dirtiness of his clothes what makes him look old, or is it the dirtiness of his *winter* clothes? It seems it would be so easy to avoid this kind of confusion. Evidently it is not.

In line 9, "butt" is out of keeping with the tone and diction of the rest of the poem. I can find no reason for this abrupt change in tone that shifts our attention from the drunk to the speaker's language. His rather formal diction, and consequently our idea of his personality and background, is suddenly disrupted.

Line 14, "being sponged," is anything but neatly said. So used, "sponged" is a grammatical impossibility. Perhaps the writer meant "absorbed," but he did not say that, and he, not I, must write his poem. (I do not want to be responsible for a chest that can absorb or act like a sponge!)

This sampling of technical problems in "Portrait" says nothing whatever about the poem's emotional meaning. It does, however, direct the author toward revisions, which, in almost every case, will require him to look at the events of his poem again, this time more closely and carefully. To revise the poem, the author will have, in an odd but real sense, to relive those events. He needs to do a lot more looking, not more thinking. From the experience of reliving the events of his poem, the author may express and discover how his characters feel about them. Like all of us, he does not know how he feels about anything until he experiences it. Writing is not only a way we communicate with others; it is a way—*the* way—we learn. (It is also the way we think. When we think about something, we talk about it to ourselves, talk in grammatical sentences.) We learn how we feel in the process of describing people and events and places to ourselves and to others. But this happens only if we direct our entire attention to what we are describing and withhold none of our energies from that task.

This collection of surprising and paradoxical statements adds up to the secret of writing. It is a secret even though all writers know it and many of them will tell it to anyone who asks. It is a secret, nevertheless, because most people are not writers and do not believe the secret no matter who tells them or no matter how many times they are told. There are more or less convincing theoretical explanations of the secret, but writers learn it from the experience of writing—the best if not the only way.

Let us see what can happen to "Portrait" if its author relives and reinvents its central experience. He sees a man get off a subway train and notice a drunk sprawled on a nearby bench. That's the situation and the plot. Anyone who has ever been in a subway, or seen a subway station on film, and who has seen or can imagine a drunk can imagine and relive the moment and so can rewrite this poem. What the scene means, what emotions description of it will express, we will know only after the poem has been written.

Go ahead. Give it a try. Relive and re-create the plot. Describe the events as if your life depended on it. Do not explain what the people think or feel. Tell us what they do, what things look like. And then have faith in whatever grows beneath your pencil. Faith that your descriptions will do all that any poem can do.

Working Late

He stepped through shuddering doors	1
Onto the empty platform,	2
Turned smartly and strode through	3
A gauntlet of tiled columns	4

From which mirrored gum machines   5
Flashed bits of his image to each other.   6

A row of red-lacquered chairs   7
Burned before him   8
In the merciless fluorescence   9
Which leached the day's stale sweetness   10
Into the echoing air.   11

On one, a dollop of tweed   12
Grew into an old coat and a stubbled face;   13
An arm beckoned,   14
No!, raised a paper bag,   15
Its mouth worked into a fringed O,   16
Toward puckering lips.   17

He *knew* what was in it   18
But slowed to hear behind him   19
A great breath drawn and released,   20
The bag filling, creases giving up their set.   21
He waited for the palm's swing,   22
The bursting, startling, deafening, POP,   23
That did not come.   24

This is an impressive piece of work on many counts. The scene in the subway station is vividly described, as is the man's remarkable fantasy that the derelict is not drinking but merely playfully blowing and popping the paper bag. While nothing is said about the man's feelings or those of the speaker, does the poem "express" their feelings? Of course it does. The poem's descriptions of what its events look like and what its people think are accurate and full enough, truthful enough, to provide the reader with a great amount of information about how its characters feel. Let me show you how I go about reading this new version.

The title, "Working Late," explains why the subway platform is "empty" (line 2). It also seems to relate to the man who leaves the train. He has been working late and is now briskly on his way home. Or, he is still working, traveling to his next appointment. But the poem allows us to relate the title to the drunk too. He is doing what for him is "work," *his* work or occupation, and it is "late" for him, as for the other man, not only because of what the clock says, but because it is "late" for all men. (Do you understand that? Try the Gospel According to St. John 9:4, "And I must work the works of him that sent me, while it is day: the night cometh, when no man can work.")

Having written the title, the author of this poem steps into the background. What follows comes to us through the perceptions of the poem's speaker. We are told that the train doors are "shuddering" (line 1). Those who have ridden subways will immediately say, "Yes, that is the truth about those doors." The words themselves move and sound like what they are describing: "shud-*d*ering *d*oors." Having been delighted by the accuracy of this detail, we read on with renewed faith in the poem's authenticity.

Line 3 tells us that the man "Turned smartly and strode through" the platform. The *way* that information is given reenacts the facts. The words themselves move "smartly," neatly, effectively, forcefully. We notice, if we wonder why the line strikes us that way, that there is alliteration: "smartly" and "strode." There is balance too, two words on each side of the "and," and each pair of words contains an initial *s* and an initial *t*. See how it makes an envelope: *T— s—* and *s— t—*. The initial *t* is repeated in the two *s* words around the "and"—"smartly" and "strode"—and there is also a musical echo of the *r* sound in each of the four words: "Turned smartly and strode through." The line gives three bursts of the *t* sound, then the related sounds, each a bit less crisp, of the *d* in "strode" and the *th* in "through." The line itself strides out of the train and across the platform! Of course we do not go through this sort of analysis when we read the poem. But our ears do! Our ears hear the sound of the words reinforce their meaning. Our ears tell us that the striding man is quick, strong, efficient. The lines tell us also that the speaker of the line, by tuning his language to the man's walk, is not only acutely perceptive, not only an able user of language, but that he is impressed with, an admirer of, the man he is describing. The walker's spirit is reinforced, emphasized, perhaps even endorsed, by the speaker. That possible endorsement

[150]

would say: this walker is quite impressive; I am moved to admiration for him, to the sincerest form of flattery—imitation. A glimpse at the speaker's feelings toward the man who leaves the train is suggested to us through this single line of the poem. Every line of a really good poem will do the same, and these glimpses add up, reinforce each other, confirm and refine each other. When we have read the entire poem, we will know a great deal about the feelings it expresses.

Having read only this far, we see the core of the poem's meaning taking shape. "Shuddering" suggests fear, danger, horror. Our striding man walks as if unaware of danger. The speaker of the poem sees both a hint of danger and the man's failure to notice it. It adds up, so far, to suggest that the speaker feels fearful for, protective of, the man who leaves the train.

The accuracy with which the subway platform is described in lines 4-6 confirms our respect for the speaker-describer. He tells the truth about the subway platform. He notices what we might miss: the reflections in the mirrors above the vending machines. It is what we would see if we looked closely enough, carefully enough. The speaker did look carefully. That means: he cares about the world he lives in. Not everybody does. Not many care as much. The tiled columns are said to form a "gauntlet," a double row between which our walker strides. The word implies danger, as in "running a gauntlet," running through parallel lines of men armed with and using weapons against one. It is the speaker who senses danger here, as he had sensed something like it in the "shuddering" of the first line. And there is a development of this feeling in the dispersion of the walker's image into "bits." Notice how the mirrored gum machines flash bits of his image "to each other." That is a conspiracy, isn't it? And yet this further expression of the speaker's fear, like everything else in the stanza, is also accurate description of the place. The sense of menace, of impending threat, is continued in the second stanza: "Burned," "merciless," "leached"(a word full of ugly overtones), "Stale," even "echoing air" (so very empty). The poem's speaker anticipates a threat to the walker, is fearful of it for him. His attitude toward the strider includes a desire to protect him, I think, although perhaps we cannot be sure of that until we read on. The drunk on the bench

[151]

sneaks up on us. At first he is not more than a "dollop," a spoonful, as in cake frosting, ice cream, or whipped cream. How striking, and oddly discomforting, is the juxtaposition of the "dollop," with its association with sweet toppings, and "tweed." The words "dollop" and "tweed" do not usually go together. Their associations, their textures, clash. Something is wrong here, the speaker feels.

The dollop grows into a derelict—a potentially dangerous fellow to come across in a deserted place. The dollop *grows!* Like a flower or like some beast in a science-fiction thriller? The context of the poem makes our answer the beast, doesn't it?

Up to this point in the poem, we have been given the speaker's view of the situation and events, an observer's view. At line 14, that outsider's view comes to correspond with the point of view of the walking man. We, the reader and the speaker, see what the man sees. We see an arm raised as if it beckoned. Then, immediately, we know we have been mistaken. That arm was not beckoning but raising a paper bag. At the end of the second stanza we all know that the drunk has a bottle of alcoholic drink in that bag. The next line (line 18) assures us that the walker knows this too. But, as the third stanza makes clear, the walker, even though he knows the man is taking a drink from that bag, believes or half-believes or hopes—there is no good word for it—that the drunk is not drinking but doing what children do with paper bags, that is, blowing them full of air in preparation for striking the bag and delighting in the great noise of the bag's rupture. Why does the walker wait for that "POP"?—he knows it will not come! How does he feel about the derelict? How does the speaker of the poem feel about the walking man's unusual behavior? The answer to that last question is the heart of the poem, what the poem is *about*.

Does the poem give us enough information so that we can answer these questions? Does this poem express feelings successfully? What feelings does it express? Let me try some answers. The speaker of the poem admires the walker, likes him, wishes him well, but is apprehensive about the dangers that surround him. There is an innocence in the walking man that we like but that may be dangerous to him—and we are worried about his ability to avoid lurking perils. Our walker is not utterly innocent. He knows, and he knows that he knows, that the drunk is simply going to take another drink. That immediately suggests that our derelict is not going to approach the walker, not going to beg him for money, threaten, or mug him. We, speaker and reader, are relieved. There is no threat. But now it dawns upon us that a threatening drunk, even a potentially violent attacker, is not the only kind of threat the scene presents. There is threat in the very *existence* of the derelict. Not a threat of personal harm, but a threat to the walking man's innocence and faith. A world that has derelicts in it can be cause for greater anguish than an attack on our person. This innocent strider through subway platforms, while seemingly un- aware of the dangers that the speaker is afraid of on his behalf, is deeply troubled by the existence of the entirely unthreatening drunk. His existence is an assault on his faith in an ideal world, an affront to his largest hopes. He is no fool, this innocent idealist. He knows that the man is drinking. But he allows himself to believe, to have faith, or hope, despite clear evidence to the contrary, that the drunk is not a drunk at all but a playful fellow, having fun with the bag as children do. He strode through the empty platform, not because he was unaware of the dangers of empty platforms at night, but because he wanted very much to think that there were no dangers, no derelicts. He *hoped* the derelict was beckoning him, hoped that there could be communi- cation between himself and the shabby man on the bench. With the last line of the poem, our walker's faith is shattered—or rather, it is not sustained. The expected "POP" does not come.

The poem goes "POP," like the bag, in that last line. In a flash, we know what we had, at most, guessed at about the walker and about the varieties of danger: personal danger at one extreme, universal danger, danger to our fellow man, to our country, to our species, to our faith in a well-ordered, just, and merciful universe, at the other.

The feelings expressed toward the walker by the speaker of this poem are much too complex to allow summary. The poem expres- ses feelings as they are felt—on the go, full of nuance, shifting in emphasis. To separate components of the speaker's emotional response, while a useful activity of analysis, is by neccesity to falsify the true nature of that response. Only the poem tells the truth. The critic's analysis, while it may help us read the poem, is itself a good deal less than the truth. Nor can the critic compete with the poem's efficiency. The poem tells its truth in twenty-four short lines; the analysis goes on and on and on, tells a distorted version of the truth, and it could, perhaps even profitably, go on much further.

How, as best as we can say it, does the speaker of the poem, feel about the man who gets off the subway train? He feels admiration, sympathy, awe. There is a touch of teasing amusement too in his response to this kind of innocence in an adult. There is wonder that such innocence exists, such faith. There is anguish at the disappointment that must come when the bag does not go "POP," anguish felt for the walker, and for us all—those who, like the speaker, had felt too little compassion for the drunk, and those who, like the walker, had felt too much.

This long discussion of "Working Late," long but much briefer than it could well have been, does not do justice to the poem's subtle richness of feeling. Nothing but the poem could be true to the poem. Nothing but the poem itself has the poem's music, its rhythm and pace, the unique flavor of its own sounds. Read the last stanza again, several times, and listen. I hear the speaker's sympathy for the walking man swell at line 23 as if he too, the speaker, had forgotten that there are derelicts on subway platforms. The speaker, too, excitedly listens for the "POP" that would mean all is well. The line celebrates that waited for, wonderful noise. And the last line mourns its absence. How abruptly the celebration ends, the voice drops: "That did not come." Thud, thud, thud, thud. Four plain monosyllables. Nothing but the poem itself is so finely tuned to the sounds of human feeling or so lovingly attentive to the world in which feelings arise. "The bag filling, creases giving up their set." That expression of the speaker's sympathy for a paper bag that is forced to conform itself to the pressure of an overwhelming internal force sounds ludicrous when I talk about it. But as an important part of the poem, its effect and its meaning strike home. It tells us a great deal about how the speaker's eye and heart confront the world.

Whether my résumé of the emotional attitudes at work in this poem strikes you as incisive or incompetent, there is no argument about the richness of the "self" the poem "expresses." The writer of the poem has used his eyes well. He has told us, in meticulous detail, about the facts of the case, the objective, physical facts. He has been true to the world of the senses and by doing so has expressed his feelings and touched ours. That he has told the truth about the facts is what made it possible for him to discover and deal with larger and invisible truths. He has told the truth about the subway platform and by doing so has been able to tell the truth about himself and all of us.

CHAPTER ELEVEN

Your Turn

We are almost done. I have told you everything you need to know—and then some. The more you know about writing poetry, the more likely you will be hesitant, even afraid of writing a poem. The chief symptom of that situation is the desire to know more and more about poetry itself—not more about how to write it but more about how to talk about writing it. Such talk can be fun, but it can also serve to keep you from doing what you came for—writing a poem. The new writers are now busily at work, writing. *You* are trying to convince youself that you need only one more bit of information before you will feel confident enough to join them. (What you really need is courage, not confidence—the courage to press on without much confidence.) I doubt that having a chance to ask questions, to get just that one last bit of information, will turn many readers into writers. But in this chapter I will give you that chance.

I suspect that those mostly pleasant and agreeable people with whom I have been talking on these pages, those people who were designed to be your representatives, have not been allowed to say everything that you yourself would have liked to say. So, here's your chance. For questions, comments, complaints, whatever, this chapter is your turn. (I hope to do some turns here too.)

***

Me: Step right up, ma'am. What is it that makes that lovely brow wrinkle?

Your Turn

Ma'am: Oh, sir, would you please tell me, if you would be so kind, when to start a new line?

Me: Certainly. It is quite simple. Look at the last word on the previous line. Once you have found that word, the rest is easy. Your very next word is the beginning of your next line.

Ma'am: Why, of course! I needn't have bothered you with such an obvious question. Thank you so much.

***

Friday

A few lines are to contain
experience:
depths, tensions,
the precipice.
But pens don't cry and paper doesn't laugh.
The volcano does not erupt on schedule,
the poem due Friday
    is a plastic Alp
        a papier-mâché mountain
    is a pot without a petunia.

***

Saying Uncle

I had an Uncle like you.
Not many cared for him,
either.
He was a hermit:
"The only person I care to get along with is me."
Like you,
He'd rant and rave to get his way.
He knew he didn't have to argue very long
with me,
but he did, anyway.
He covered his feelings with what looked like scorn,

took pride in being "one of a kind."
That's why
I've never told you this before.
(He never liked flowers.)
That's why
I come empty-handed
With these memories.

***

Ma'am: It's me again, sir, the lady who asked you where to begin a new line.

Me: Hello again. Did you figure it out?

Ma'am: Not really. It is just as hard to know where a line should end as it is to know where a line should begin.

Me: I guess it is. Perhaps you are also unsure about spaces between lines and between words, and about when to use capital letters, and when not.

Ma'am: Yes, all of those. And when to use punctuation marks. Some of the good poems leave them out.

Me: Do you play the piano, ma'am?

Ma'am: Oh yes.

Me: Good. How do you know when to play fast, when to play soft, or to pause, or to use the pedal? The music tells you, doesn't it? The marks on the paper are directions that tell you these things. I don't mean only the musical signs that say what the rhythm and tempo should be, the loud and soft symbols, the explicit directions about pedal and pizzicato. I mean the notes too. As you play them you come to learn more exactly how the piece goes. Not only slow or fast, loud or soft, but *exactly* how much of each. The notes themselves tell you *exactly* how long to pause, how quickly to ripple a chord. The marks on the paper that a writer makes, the words and the mechanical signs, are very much like that. The composer uses his marks so you will play the piece the way he wants it played. The poet uses his marks so that you will read his poem the way he wants it read. Nobody tells the composer when to write it loud, or soft, or whatever. That's up to him. The composer, I suppose, does it by trial and error. He writes

[158]

a piece of music, then plays it as he wrote it. If it sounds right, he's done. If not, he changes it. Write your line and read it back to yourself. Does it sound right? Good. Does it sound wrong? Too slow, too fast, too loud, the pause too short or too long? Listen again to be sure. Then change the words, the spaces between them, the size and place of the letters, the punctuation, whatever there is to change. Some of the marks you can make on your paper may not seem to affect the way the poem is read—like capital letters, for instance. But big or small letters, long or short lines, spaces and punctuation, at least change the way the poem looks to your eye. If you like the way it looks, fine. If not, change the way it looks. That's all there is to it. There are no rules.

Ma'am: What if it doesn't make any difference to the way my line sounds or looks—changing it, that is?

Me: If it doesn't make any difference, then it doesn't make any difference. Except that it always makes a difference. You have to look and listen harder in order to tell the difference. If you still can't, you are finished with that line. Perhaps you will see differences when you have assembled a group of lines and can look and listen to them together. That's the whole story. That's all there is; there ain't no more.

***

Me: You're leaving?

Sunny: Don't you see, the sun is out, shining.

Me: I *had* noticed.

Sunny: Well, I'm going out for some fun. No offense. I think it's wonderful what people can do with poetry, but I want a swim and a tan and some fun.

Me: But if you go, who will write the poems, who will read them? We all need you.

Sunny: Oh, there are plenty of others.

Me: Oh, no. We need you, and *they* need you. Is it really so wonderful to be out in the sunshine?

Sunny: Try it!

Me: I did.

***

[159]

How to Write a Poem

The Old Motor Scooter

who gives a damn
about

an old motor
scooter

sweating brown
rust

behind the "Chicken
Delight"?

You: What's all that about?

Me: It is a parody of, a sort of tribute to, a very famous poem. Didn't you know?

You: No. Should I have known the "very famous" poem?

Me: Certainly. And you will know it if you continue to learn about poetry. But don't you like the motor scooter poem anyhow? Isn't it pleasant to listen to and to look at?

You: Yes, it *is.* But it's hard to like something you don't understand.

Me: Of course it's hard, but we do it all the time. And this poem is easy to like and to answer. It is a one-sentence question. Who cares about a scooter rusting in the back yard? Who cares about the pleasant way the question itself is asked? Who cares about the lovely, shaped language and the thrill of "sweating brown / rust"? Do you know the answer?

You: Poets?

Me: Yes, *all* the good guys.

***

Excuse me, sir. I'm leaving too. I have read everything so far— the rules, the examples, the discussions. What you say sounds reasonable enough most of the time, but the poems you call failures strike me as pretty good. The poems you like, like this silly

[160]

business about a motor scooter, I find confusing, affected, and disagreeable. My own attempts at poetry please me and the educated people I show them to. Both my wife and my daughter teach English, and both tell me my poems are quite good. I have had several of them published. But I have no doubt you would despise my poems, and I will not give you that pleasure. Good day.

***

Pretty Young Thing: Is this a good poem?

What Are You Thinking?

what are you thinking?
you furrow your brow and i try to read you—
as i would a book
you stare into space, drowsy-eyed
your lashes half-closed over your tired
green cat's eyes

you turn,
look at the wall behind me—
slowly, in a dream,
you focus for a moment,
but i can't read you
because your glasses reflect the light
from the Bud commercial behind the bar
and all i see is the smiling girl,
holding the foaming mug,
and smeared fingerprints on your lenses.

i want to take your face in my hands
to explore the lines and stubble,
to look deep into those drowning pools of green,
to see into you, to your innermost part
and to read your story.

what are you thinking?

How to Write a Poem

deep in contemplation you are oblivious
to the band
pouring out its rhythm

on

and on

and on

you wiggle like a puppy
suddenly aware of being watched.
are you trying to escape me?

finally
our eyes meet and i hold you.
you stare a moment, confused?
then you smile slowly, sleepily and
i return your smile

but

i still wonder, as the band drones on

what story do you have to tell?

Thing: Is it a good poem?
Me: Not very.
Thing: Would you please fix it for me?
Me: I didn't say it was *broken.*
Thing: Well, could you improve it, make it a good poem?
Me: I'm sorry. That's against my principles. If I fixed it, whose
poem would it be? Not exactly yours anymore.
Thing: It would be better. It would be *ours!*
Me: Who could resist? Here:

What Are You Thinking?
(our version)

You furrow your brow.
What are you thinking?
I try to read you,
your stare, drowsy-eyed,
lashes half-closed over your tired green cat's eyes.

[162]

Your Turn

You turn,
look at the wall behind me,
and focus for a moment.
Your glasses reflect
the Bud sign behind the bar.
I see the smiling girl holding a foaming mug,
and fingerprints on your lenses.
But I can't read you.

I want to take your face in my hands,
explore the lines and stubble,
look deep into those drowning pools of green.

Thing: Go *on.*
Me: That's it. Isn't it better?
Thing: You left out *half* of it!
Me: I put it all in, at least I tried to. Your poem was shorter than you thought. There was less poem in it than you thought.
Thing: You left out the band, and the puppy, and the ending.
Me: But I put in what mattered, just took out the air, the soft stuff, that was getting in the way. Don't you like it better now?
Thing: No.
Me: Isn't it *our* poem?
Thing: It's yours. Mine was the *longer* one.
Me: Shallower.
Thing: How could you!
Me: How could *you?*
Thing: I tried to read *you!* Didn't you know?
Me: I hoped so, but evidently you couldn't.
Thing: Get a shave!

***

Curious: You never explained what a metaphor is?
Me: A metaphor is a comparison.
Curious: Then what is a simile, and a metonymy?
Me: And then you will want to know about personification, synecdoche, tropes, appositives, hyperbole, or are you just trying to find out if I know these words? There are many kinds of meta-

phors, and names for each kind. And there are hundreds of other technical terms in literature. They can be useful for advanced critics and theorists, but they are most commonly used as instruments for the torture of children. They make it possible for teachers who know nothing about literature to fill their time, to bore their charges, and to grade examinations in the safest and least time-consuming manner. A metaphor is a comparison. That is all you know—and all you need to know.

Curious: My literature textbooks say these things are very important.

Me: Throw them away!

***

The Lesson

Good poetry does not rhyme
But that's not this poem's only crime.
The meter is simply sing-song
And that's not the only thing that's wrong,
The meaning—it's all too unclear,
Obviously this poet's insincere
And his words are spent with too much ease—
I'm afraid his poem will not please.

You may think me rude or rash
But this poem is a piece of trash;
The writer wrote it for himself
To join the pile upon his shelf.
This precious little piece of you
Is what a ten-year-old might do.

This man here didn't sign his name—
It's a lousy poem just the same.
Don't you know this is the big time;
You came here, the choice wasn't mine.
And if you don't like what I say,
Feel free to get up and walk away.

Your Turn

Feel miserable rather, at giving up,
Whine and howl you rhyming pup.

***

What's good is what *you* like! The more we do what you tell us
to do, the worse we write. You *love* that! What you like most is
telling us we're no good after you've tricked us into writing poorly.
Sadist! Smiling Sadist!

***

Apology

I'm sorry, sir.
You were so interested in me
Last night at the party.
We sat on the arms
Of the same great green chair.
You told your tale,
Listened to mine.
You looked so vulnerable.
Behind gold-rimmed frames
Your droopy liquid-blue eyes,
Stroked my face.
Wild curly brown hair
Shook with the gestures of your
Story.
Please forgive a young woman
Whose young man is far away.

***

What about rhyme? What about rhyme? It used to have to
rhyme.
   Me: Indeed it did. Used to. It don't no more.
   Rhymer: Sez who?
   Me: Sez 'most everybody, and have for fifty year. Don't got to
scan neither.

Rhymer: Scan? What's scan?
Me: Like this:

I wish I were away from here.
Among the folks who'll shed a tear

(Ĭ wísh Ĭ wére ă-wáy frŏm hére

Ă-móng thĕ fólks whŏ'll shéd ă teár)

di-da di-da di-da di-da
di-da di-da di-da di-da

Four di-da's in each line. It rhymes and it scans!
Enthusiast: Oh, I know! Iambic tetrameter.
Me: Yes, rhymed iambic tetrameter. Iambic for di-da, and there's four of them for tetrameter. But the lines sound like the beginning of a dreadful poem.
Enthusiast: I like them. And it is "there *are* four of them," not "there is" or "there's." Somebody like you ought to know better.
Me: I do, that's how's come I can. If I can, I can, and if it works, I will.
Rhymer: I don't think it worked, sir. She's gone off in a funk, sir.
Me: You did it again!

Í dŏn't thínk ĭt wórked, sĭr

Shĕ's góne ŏff ín ă fúnk, sĭr

Rhymed, an identical rhyme it's called. And this is trochaic trimeter with initial variation in the second line, feminine endings, and an internal slant rhyme ("wor*k*ed" and "fun*k*"). See how easy it is!
Rhymer: I didn't know I had it in me.
Me: You did. You got rhythm, and I got fancy names to call it. I'd take the rhythm if I had a choice—and I doooOOOOOOO.
Rhymer:

Your Turn

She's a'coming back, I see her yellin'
She's goin' t' 'plain about yo' spellin'

Me: Let's scram.
Rhymer: Hot damn.
Me: 'Round that bend.
Rhymer: Sure 'nuff, friend.

***

Sheets

I think another thought will never come.
("It is not thoughts, but things.")
My heartbeat pounds:
Think think   think think   think things!
(Have I lost it, am I dry?)

The scent of roses on the night table distracts;
Thoughts drift into wrinkled sheets,
Wet with tears and love.
And ink.

***

Next: You tell us to make it up and you tell us to tell the truth. That sounds like a contradiction. How can I do both things at once?

Me: If you don't understand how, and if it will make you more comfortable, you have my permission to disregard whichever instructions you prefer. Either tell the truth *or* make it up. Okay?

Next: It's just that I want to understand what poetry is.

Me: Everybody wants to and nobody does. Despite that, poems get written and read.

Next: I want to be sincere, and making it up sounds insincere.

Me: Well, don't make it up, tell the truth.

Next: But I don't know what the truth is.

Me: Well, pretend that you do. Make it up.

[167]

How to Write a Poem

Next: That would be insincere. I don't like to do that.

Me: But *you* and what you *want* have very little to do with writing poems. Poems get written when a writer becomes so interested in someone or something outside himself that he is obsessed with it. He does not choose. He is *forced* to pay attention to, and to find words for, what it is that has seized his imagination. Unless or until that happens, nothing happens. What the writer wants, whether it is to be sincere, or to write a good poem, or to win a prize, is utterly irrelevant. Worse than irrelevant. To want to write a poem, to want *anything*, is a surefire way to *not* write a good poem.

Next: But I want . . .

Me: No want's, no but's.

Next: But I . . .

Me: Next!

***

For L. J. D.

You told us to be precise
to tell it like it is
or as we see it or imagine it

but, you know, sometimes I
just don't see nothing.
and sometimes words can't
explain what things I see before me;

The garbage cans clang in the morning,
the sun blinds me on the way home from work,
in the car with all four of its wheels
on the ground at the same time;

The wind blows my hair into
a crazy shape
on top
of my head

Your Turn

You told us to center
in on one small detail:
the crease in a rose
petal
the cigarette ashes lying
in a corner;
You told us to stay away
from generalities and abstractions,
not to talk about
the abyss, the one that will come some day,
or reality,
or someone out there—
bring him in here where
we can see him you said;

But life isn't like
that; it rains and snows
and people get flat tires
and their poodles die and
people lose their lovers.

They look out the window
and cry,
smoke cigarettes.

***

Weepy: Oh, oh, please, please, don't go. Please read mine!
Me: Is it any good?
Weepy: I hope so; I think so. Almost good.
Me: You read it. Take a long breath, and read it for all it's worth, as if it were immensely valuable, each syllable of it. Go!

(Untitled)

Pushing.   Pushing.
A cataclysm of spasms throws the inner
     swimmer forward, driving it out.

[169]

Again.   And again.   And again.
   And again.
The intensity of the waves slam it to the edge.
It surges outward, cleaving the plum-rose walls
And emerges, a new life,
Glistening and slick, to be cradled in the
      soft white-banked thighs.

Weepy: What do you think of it?
Me: It is on the verge of being terrific. If you had more
confidence in it you wouldn't have let it collapse at the end, and
you would have trusted it more, trusted it to stand alone, without
the padding, the nervous explanations. And it cries for a title.
Weepy: (Weepy.)
Me: I *said* it was almost terrific, and it is. Terrific plus scared
equals almost terrific. Shall I take out what needs taking out?
Weepy: Pleeeese.

Pushing.   Pushing.
A cataclysm throws the inner
swimmer forward,
drives it out,
Again.   And again.   And again.
   And again.
Waves slam it to the lips.
It surges outward,
Cleaving the plum-rose walls,
and emerges,
glistening and slick.

Me: See? I told you it was terrific. And I have a title for it that
knocks me out.
Weepy: "Birth"?
Me: No. Not at all. Your poem describes something else in the
terms of a birth. Birth is used as a metaphor, a comparison, in
order to describe better something else, something nearer to you,
to us, to the experience of grown-up life. Three guesses. The poem
is about you, about what is very important to you.

[170]

Weepy: Tell me.

Me: It is an autobiographical poem. Very true, very serious, and with two puns: "lips" and "slick." Now you know.

Weepy: (A gasp, a groan, and a desperate sigh.) I'm so embarrassed!

Me: And proud too, I hope. And not so embarrassed either. Terrific poem.

Weepy: Thank you, thank you.

Me: See you around.

Hey, wait. Aren't you going to tell us the title?

Me: Wait just a minute, until she's out the door. No sense making her more embarrassed than she is. Okay. The title is: "First Poem."

***

Polly: My mother always says: "If you can't say something nice, don't say anything at all."

Me: That's nice.

Polly: But you want us to write about pain and trouble and fear. Unless it's sad you call it trivial.

Me: I usually do. I'm sorry.

Polly: Why does it have to be unhappy to be good?

Me: That's a good question. I don't know the answer. It's not *my* fault. I don't like dying anymore than you do.

Polly: And that's what the poems you like best are about— death.

Me: Very true. About death, and against it, and despite it.

CHAPTER TWELVE

Publishing

There is nothing that feels quite so good as having a publisher or editor write you to say that your poem has been accepted. How strange and wonderful it is to see your words, and your name, printed in type, in a book or magazine. Congratulations. Enjoy it. You are now, by definition, a poet. You are no longer the only one who thinks so.

You will, I hope, not let your success go to your head. While it is conceivable that your editor is a person of impeccable judgment, you may find that his other choices, the other poems printed in the magazine that contains your masterpiece, are uneven—or worse. What, you may ask, is my poem doing in this company? You might consider the possibility that you are likely to admire your own work with a special affection. You might remind yourself that editors, however conscientious, can select only from what they are offered. They have pages to fill, deadlines to meet, subscribers to please.

How editors go about their business is one of those questions about which ignorance is widespread. That ignorance you will be wise to consider bliss. Even if you know the editor personally— even if he is deeply indebted to you—his actions will probably be utterly unpredictable. Neither the back issues of the magazine, nor its statements about editorial policies, nor its rejection notices and explanations will be of the slightest use in predicting the fate of your next submission. No amount of research into the magazine's ownership or purpose, or into the editor's private or professional life, will tell you what you want to know. Look at the selection process as a lottery and save yourself the turmoil of trying to outguess the enigma.

While one would think that a neatly typed manuscript is a basic requirement, experience may lead you to believe that a grease stain, or an outworn typewriter ribbon, is the secret key to acceptance. Some editors, I suspect, are susceptible, at some moments of their days, to teardrops on manuscripts. Bloodstains, charred edges, postscripts bearing threats of suicide or homicide—editors, like traffic court judges and college teachers, have heard everything before. That does not mean that they are immune to unusual approaches, but you can never tell what their particular weak spots are. They will certainly never tell you. You will never know whether their judgments are based on reason or on whimsy. Don't even try to find out.

Most poets send their work to periodicals: literary monthlies or quarterlies, magazines that print only poetry, and general magazines of an intellectual cast that print a few pages of poetry each issue. A few magazines pay, modestly, for the poems they use. It would be wise not to expect those magazines to accept work from unknown writers. Most poetry magazines, in which celebrated names appear alongside the unfamiliar, pay their contributors in the form of copies, typically two copies, of the magazine. There are hundreds, perhaps thousands, of such magazines. Some are sponsored by colleges and universities and edited by boards of poets and professors. Some are sponsored by private individuals or small groups and are edited by whoever has been paying the printing bill. Some poetry journals have appeared regularly for decades; some appear when the owner-operator is in the mood to go down to the basement and crank up the mimeograph machine. These categories are not exhaustive. There are magazines edited and printed by private individuals that are scrupulously edited, printed, and managed. There are university-sponsored magazines that are a scandal. There are, believe it or not, poetry magazines that never appear. Perhaps the owner has noble intentions, a desire to provide a forum for writing of a kind and quality he thinks other publications are wrong to shun. Perhaps the owner has been overcome by his vision of himself as an editor. Whatever the intention, something goes wrong and you may see ads soliciting submissions—even selling subscriptions—to magazines whose names appear in directories of publishers, but that never appear. You may receive printed rejection slips from such magazines. You may receive detailed criticism of your work or be encouraged to submit more poems. Your poem may be accepted—but you will wait forever to see it in print. These cases are rare but not at all unheard of.

The only things all the poetry magazines have in common is that none of them operates at a monetary profit, and none of them has any official standing. The magazines report to no superior or licensing body. They are not responsible to the general public in the ways a profit-making business is. There is no place to appeal their decisions or to demand that they publish—or even return—the poems you have sent them. Whenever you submit poems to a magazine, you are putting yourself in the hands of an unknown and unregulated power.

If you live near one of our country's great cities or great universities, you can find a bookstore that displays and sells a selection of poetry magazines, or a library in which you may examine many of them. Public libraries in smaller cities often carry a few, as do libraries and bookstores in smaller college towns. Very often, a single poetry magazine will carry advertisements for several others, and the names of yet others will appear in the biographical sketches of the contributors. Directories of small publishers can provide addresses for magazines whose names you come to know. Librarians have guides to periodicals that list and describe poetry magazines. Many magazines go in and out of existence often, so do not be surprised if your submissions come back from "Address Unknown." You can subscribe to poetry magazines whose names you know. If you have a favorite poet, his books will probably give the names of periodicals in which his work first appeared. It would seem wise to write for a subscription to a few of the magazines, or for a single recent copy or back number. There are so many poetry magazines, however, that it is not uncommon for a writer to submit poems to a magazine he has never seen. When you find a poetry magazine whose work you like and find comparable to your own, go out and buy some postage stamps. Unless the magazine itself says otherwise, here are the rules of the game:

1. Do not write to inquire about the magazine's editorial policy or to ask if they would like to see some of your poems.

2. Assemble neat, original, typewritten copies of two to four of your poems. Your name and address should appear on every page you send.

3. Write a letter to the magazine's editor offering him, or her, or them, the poems. If you don't know the editor's name, call him "Dear Editor." Your letter can go like this: "I submit for your consideration my poems entitled. . . ." Then write: "SASE enclosed." Date your letter. Make and file a carbon copy of it and the poems.

4. Prepare a self-addressed stamped envelope (SASE). That is, a standard business envelope, 9½ by 4¼, addressed to yourself, with a stamp in the top right-hand corner. Fold it in thirds, the long way, and put it in another standard envelope addressed to the editor. Insert your letter and your poems and affix sufficient postage. If your letter weighs more than the minimum amount, put the correct amount of postage on both the outer envelope and the SASE. A postage scale is needed, or your post office will weigh the letter for you and figure the amount of stamps needed.

5. Until the poems are rejected and returned to you, do not submit them to another publication.

There are no standard rules for editors. Some publications acknowledge receipt of your poems with a postcard and give some indication of the number of months it will take them to reach a decision. Most do neither. If you have had no response after five or six months, you can write again, asking for a status report. Editors of poetry magazines are often overworked and underpaid, if paid at all. They are busy with other obligations. They seem to take long vacations, especially in the summer. (One or two revel in bohemian irresponsibility.) They may accumulate hundreds of letters, like yours, in a few weeks, after a full moon, and, try as they may, embarrassed as they may be about it, your letter may remain unopened for months. A courteous letter of inquiry may be the prod they need. (Put your return address on the front of all your envelopes so that the editors can find it if they want to.) I have heard of people who believe that a letter of inquiry, meticulously phrased to express rage or solicitude or pathetic innocence, can so embarrass an editor that he will accept the poems, sight unseen, out of remorse. Don't count on it. If you get no response to your letter of inquiry after a month or so, you have several options. You may believe that your editor is dead or dying, his hand wedged forever in the mimeograph machine. You may believe that he earns his living by steaming stamps off SASEs. If you are sufficiently enraged or curious, you may consider calling him on the telephone. (Announce yourself as some very famous poet—or the police.)

Whatever you do, the rules say this: when your patience is exhausted, write once more asking the editor to return your poems and advising him that you are withdrawing the submission. Then you are free to submit the poems elsewhere. Do not spend too much time wondering whether your negligent editor has beat you to it and has submitted *your* poems to another magazine under *his* name. This is a rare event, if it happens at all, but quite common as a subject of nightmares. The probabilities are that your poems will come back to you in a few weeks or months in your SASE accompanied by a printed rejection slip. It is widely believed that magazines have a number of different rejection slips, each version conveying, in a secret code, their real opinion of your work. If the slip says, "Sorry. But thanks for letting us see your work," it may indicate more—or less—respect for the work than a slip that says, "The editors have not found this material suitable for their needs." A handwritten "Sorry" is prized by some writers, as are the very common rejection slips on which is printed, "but please let us see more examples of your work." This last version would seem to be the sign of the stamp collector, although the wording appears on slips from prestigious publications. I do not recommend taking them at their word and introducing your next submission to them by saying, "In response to your request to see more of my poems, here are. . . ."

Publishing

Keep buying stamps. Sooner or later you may find an editor who likes and accepts your poems. Until this happens, each rejection slip should be taken as a kind of encouragement. It is healthy to take it as evidence that there are people who care about poetry and about standards of quality. A rejection slip means that someone has probably read your poem. It tells you what you probably knew yourself: you must do better. If you think you can, you will, and one day your SASE will come back to you, thinner and lighter than your original letter. Your poems have been kept! (If it is any comfort to you, until then, remember that famous poets continue to get rejection slips, even Pulitzer Prize and National Book Award winners.)

After you write the editor to acknowledge his letter of acceptance and to supply the biographical information he requested, you may expect to receive your two copies of *your* magazine within anywhere from a few weeks to eighteen months. Usually you will be told at the time of acceptance what issue will have the honor of introducing your poem or poems to the world, but bear in mind that the "Spring" issue is the one that says "Spring" on the cover. Wait till September before inquiring for it. (Yes, it is possible, if unlikely, that your publisher will go out of business before issuing the Spring number.)

(Two copies of the magazine that published my own debut arrived promptly. My pleasure at this long-awaited triumph was somewhat reduced by seeing that the author's name—my name—had been mysteriously changed from "Lawrence" to "James." I complained and was advised to make sure that my name appeared on each page of manuscript I submitted. The magazine's next issue, in which more of my work appeared, the first acceptance having been for a rather lengthy group of poems, ran this explanatory note: "Lawrence Dessner appeared in our last issue as James Dessner." An unusual apology! No doubt readers of that magazine wondered what name I would use next time. The moral of the story: expect editors to do the incomprehensible.)

Your new status as a published poet will be remarkably similar to your earlier condition. "Poets" who write rock-and-roll lyrics or who strike exotic poses in films and avant-garde magazines, or who are seen in advertisements for expensive things, are not reliable guides to your immediate expectations. Fan mail is exceedingly rare. Mail of any sort in response to your publication should not be expected. The world will continue to revolve with undiminished regularity. Nor is it even sure that your next submissions will receive more friendly treatment if you tell the editors of your previous publications. You are free to tell them, of course, but this is very difficult to do gracefully. What effect your new credentials will have on editors is anybody's guess.

As your acceptances mount up—and of course as your poems get better—you will want to consider the typical next step: a book of poems, both new ones and the best of those already published. The simplest, most prestigious, but, alas, least promising course is to invite a leading commercial publisher to read and publish your manuscript. Do not send one of these publishers your unsolicited manuscript unless you are prepared to wait a long time for a reply. Do not expect to get it back at all unless you send along stamps to pay for its return. Write first, describing your work and your publishing record, and ask if they want to see your manuscript. If they do, they will tell you so—using their own stamps. The worst they can say is no. No answer at all, after six weeks, means no. But you can send letters of inquiry to more than one publisher at the same time. There are many competitions, which are announced in poetry magazines, for which the prize is book publication. There are hundreds of small publishers, or presses, that publish poetry volumes in elegant if poorly distributed editions. These tend to be profit-sharing ventures—that means loss-sharing—but they need not be dismissed out of hand for that reason. The literary arts have had a long history of private patronage. But make sure with whom you are dealing. There are sharks in these waters too.

An author can choose to become his own publisher. That is, he contracts for the printing and manufacture of his book and takes upon himself the many chores of sales, publicity, shipping, and so on. Your librarian, or a local job printer, can introduce you to one of the comprehensive guidebooks to what is called "Self-Publishing." There is no reason to disdain this possibility, as long as you can afford the initial investment—afford, that is, to lose most of it. In the long run, the world will decide how good a poet you are. Aside from writing well, all *you* have to do is give the world a

Publishing

reasonable chance to find you. In the short run, reputations, even in the nonprofit art of poetry, can be made by shrewd, lucky, and reprehensible self-advertisement. A press agent will tell you all about it. See the Yellow Pages, and bring your checkbook.

The most aggressive competitors for your book-publishing dollar are the "vanity presses." Some of them are outright frauds. The best are responsible and reliable, although their sales techniques are obnoxious. They will publish *anything*—and why not? The author, their customer, takes all the risks. But they produce attractive-looking books and do some promotion and advertising. Once in a blue moon a vanity press book breaks even or makes money or a reputation. This is the longest of long shots. If you want to have a book of your own poems to give to friends and relatives, and to send to other poets and to commercial publishers, by all means pay to have it printed. Printed, not published. Your local printing firm that produces commercial books and pamphlets for business and institutional customers can do the job for you at surprisingly low cost.

A word may need to be said about matchbook covers anxious to set your poem to music. On no account should you offer to relieve their anxiety.

Alert readers of classified advertisements in general magazines or of bulletin boards in college English departments will have noticed invitations to submit poetry for an anthology, "soon to be published." Believe it or not, some of these offers are legitimate, if probably misguided, operations. In some cases, an aspiring person of letters, a would-be editor or publisher, becomes one by running and paying for his own anthology. A sort of vanity editing. Contributors may be paid, but are more likely to be asked for $10 or $20 for their copies of the anthology. Sometimes an elaborate procedure of selection and an imposing list of advisory editors are part of the process. Even so, the best place to spend your money is at the stamp window of the post office. And your best bet for an informed and intelligent appraisal of your poetry is that enigmatic editor of poetry magazines. Good luck. Keep those editors busy. It will keep you writing, and rewriting, and trying harder, and getting better.

Postscript

Me: Well, good-bye. It's been nice talking to you.

You: Is that it?

Me: Wasn't it enough? There were times your face told me it was more than enough.

You: Sorry about that. It's just that I'll miss my coach. Who can I show my poems to?

Me: There are always editors, such as they are, and English teachers, some of them. The library is full of silent but very good coaches, and there are people very much like yourself.

You: The problem is there aren't enough people who can read poetry or want to.

Me: These are, as usual, hard times for poetry.

You: It seems that the only people who can read poems write them.

Me: Write them for a while at least, until they reach and know their limits. It is no small feat to recognize the genius of other people and submit to it.

You: What we need is more readers of poetry.

Me: A nation of good readers! That is the only hope, the oldest utopia. Well, go out there and spread the word. It's your turn.

You: Do you think the Dark Ages are coming back?

Me: They never left. The miracle is that there is any light at all. The more our light shines, the more we are the target. Be careful. Let me know how you make out. And thanks for all your help.

[180]

APPENDIX A

The Rules

1. Write a poem.
2. Respect your reader.
3. Respect yourself.
4. Be specific.
5. Find your own language.
6. Read other people's poems.
7. When in doubt, leave it out.
8. Make it up.
9. A poem must have a hero.
10. Grow up.

The Rule of Rules: Tell the Truth.

APPENDIX B

The Questionnaires

The Hero: Name
Date and place of birth
Education, formal and informal
Religious background and practice
Occupational history
Income
Marital status and history
Social class
Economic class
Ethnic background
Residence
Automobile
Hobbies
Physique and facial appearance
Philosophy of life
Hopes
Prospects
Personality
Siblings
Spouse and Parents: occupation
education
income
etc.
Etc.

The Place: Date—year, month, day
Time—hour, minute

[183]

The Questionnaires

Weather—temperature, humidity, wind, sky, etc.
Location—city, neighborhood, street
  Interior—furnishings, lighting, windows, etc.
  Exterior—terrain, vegetation, vistas
Clothing and adornment
Odors
Sounds
Tastes and textures

The Point: Why is the hero in this place?
  What does he hope to find or accomplish there?
  What does being in this place mean to him?
  What is he about to learn?

APPENDIX C

Reading Contemporary Poetry

A list of good paperback books:

Allen, Donald M., ed. *The New American Poetry.* Grove Press, 1960.

Berg, Stephen, and Robert Mezey, eds. *Naked Poetry: Recent American Poetry in Open Forms.* Bobbs-Merrill, 1969.

Carruth, Hayden, ed. *The Voice That Is Great Within Us: American Poetry of the Twentieth Century.* Bantam, 1970.

Ellmann, Richard and Robert O'Clair, eds. *The Norton Anthology of Modern Poetry.* Norton, 1973.

Hall, Donald, ed. *Contemporary American Poetry.* Penguin, 1971.

Hall, Donald, Robert Pack, and Louis Simpson, eds. *New Poets of England and America.* Meridian, 1957.

Halpern, Daniel, ed. *The American Poetry Anthology.* Equinox-Avon, 1975.

Hollander, John, ed. *Poems of Our Moment: Contemporary Poets of the English Language.* Pegasus, 1968.

Leary, Paris, and Robert Kelly, eds. *A Controversy of Poets: An Anthology of Contemporary American Poetry.* Anchor, 1965.

Lee, Al, ed. *The Major Young Poets.* Meridian, 1971.

Monaco, Richard, ed. *New American Poetry.* McGraw-Hill, 1973.

Poulin, A., Jr., ed. *Contemporary American Poetry.* Houghton Mifflin, 1975.

Strand, Mark, ed. *The Contemporary American Poets: American Poetry Since 1940.* Mentor, 1969.

Williams, Miller, ed. *Contemporary Poetry in America.* Random House, 1973.